The Pocket Guide to
AIRLINE
MARKINGS
and
Commercial Aircraft

First English edition published by Temple Press
an imprint of Newnes Books 1985

This 1985 edition published by Gallery Books
an imprint of W.H. Smith Publishers Inc.

Produced by David Donald
Aerospace Publishing Ltd
179 Dalling Road
London W6 0ES

Contributors: John Roach
                David Mondey

© Aerospace Publishing Ltd 1985
Colour profiles © Pilot Press Ltd

First published 1985
Reprinted 1986, 1988

All correspondence concerning the content of this volume
should be addressed to Aerospace Publishing Ltd. Trade
enquiries should be addressed to W.H. Smith Publishers
Inc, 112 Madison Avenue, New York, New York 10016.

ISBN 0-8317-7019-8

Printed in Hong Kong by Mandarin Offset

The Pocket Guide to
AIRLINE
MARKINGS
and
Commercial Aircraft
Editor: David Donald

GALLERY BOOKS
An Imprint of W. H. Smith Publishers Inc.
112 Madison Avenue
New York City 10016

Contents

Airlines

Aircraft

Aer Lingus

Aer Lingus was formed on 22 May 1936 and initially operated a de Havilland D.H.84 Dragon between Dublin and Bristol. In 1947 Aerlinte Eireann was formed to operate transatlantic services, and operations finally began on 28 April 1958. The two airlines' services are now intergrated. Aer Lingus was the first airline in the world to take delivery of the Fokker F.27 Friendship Mk 100 on 19 November 1958. The airline's BAC One-Eleven 208ALs (delivered from May 1965) and Boeing 737-248s (delivered from April 1969) operate an extensive network of scheduled passenger and cargo services from Dublin, Shannon and Cork to 11 cities in the UK and to 13 points in Europe. The Boeing 747s are used for charters and leasing work, plus scheduled services to New York and Boston. A recently formed division Aer Lingus Commuter operates Shorts 360s within Eire and to points in the UK. The major shareholder is the Irish government. Associate companies are Irish Helicopters, Aviation Traders, Airmotive Ireland and Guinness Peat Aviation/Air Tara.

Fleet:
BAC One-Eleven
Boeing 737

Boeing 747
Shorts 360

Aer Lingus' Boeing 747s are used primarily on long-haul routes to the United States but are available for charter and leasing work.

Aermediterranea

Formed on 20 March 1981 as a subsidiary of Alitalia, Aermediterranea was created to take over from Aerolinee Itavia. Operations started on 1 July 1981 with Douglas DC-9-32s transferred from Alitalia. Major shareholders are Alitalia (55 per cent) and Aero Trasporti Italiani (45 per cent). Currently the airline employs approximately 400 staff. The airline operates its all DC-9 fleet on charter services within Europe (mainly to Germany and the United Kingdom), scheduled services within Italy from Milan to Alghero, Catania, Lanezia, Palermo and Pisa, and from Rome (Fiumicino) to Bologna, Lamezia Pisa and Verona.

Fleet:
Douglas DC-9-32

Aeroflot

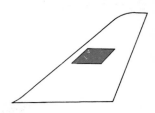

The origin of Aeroflot, the world's largest airline, can be traced back to an airline that commenced operations in 1921, namely Deruluft, a Soviet-German company. The airline's current name was adopted in 1932. Aeroflot, unlike many other airlines, introduced a pure jet airliner into service before a turboprop aircraft, this being the Tupolev Tu-104 on 15 September 1956. Aeroflot's biggest expansion was between 1959 and 1963, when the Antonov An-10 and An-24, Ilyushin Il-18, Tupolev Tu-114 and Tu-124 all entered service. The Soviet airline was the first in the world to launch services with a supersonic transport, the Tupolev Tu-144, on 26 December 1975. Aeroflot currently employs between 400,000 and 500,000 staff. Scheduled passenger and cargo services are operated on an enormous network of domestic routes plus international services to North, South and Central America, Europe, Africa, and the Middle and Far East. Other major areas of work carried outby the airline are agriculture, fishery, survey and ice reconnaissance, Antarctic and Arctic expedition support, anti-forest fire-patrol and aeromedical services. On the short domestic routes Aeroflot uses the Yakovlev Yak-40, An-24, Tu-134, Let L-410UVP and An-28; on short and medium routes the Yak-42 and wide-bodied Il-86 and Tu-154 are operated; and on long-haul and many international routes Aeroflot uses the Il-62.

Fleet:

Antonov An-2
Antonov An-12
Antonov An-24
Antonov An-26
Antonov An-30
Antonov An-72
Ilyushin Il-14
Ilyushin Il-18
Ilyushin Il-62
Ilyushin Il-76
Ilyushin Il-86

Kamov Ka-26
Kamov Ka-32
Let L-410
Mil Mi-2
Mil Mi-6
Mil Mi-8
Mil Mi-10
Tupolev Tu-134
Tupolev Tu-154
Yakovlev Yak-40
Yakovlev Yak-42

Aeroflot's most numerous international type is the Tupolev Tu-154. These are used throughout Europe and Asia on both scheduled and charter work.

7

The Soviet Union's first wide-body airliner was the Ilyushin Il-86, capable of carrying up to 350 passengers on high-density routes in the Soviet Union. The type is also used on long-range and high-density sectors internationally.

Aerolineas Argentinas

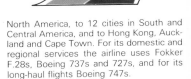

Formed on 14 May 1949 by the Ministry of Transport, Aerolineas Argentinas took over from four smaller airlines (FAMA, ALFA, Aeroposta and ZONDA) whose origins can be traced back to 1928, FAMA began services to London with Douglas DC-4s on 17 September 1946. The airline's first jet service, with a de Havilland Comet 4, was on 19 May 1958 between Buenos Aires and London. The first Boeing 747 was delivered on 16 December 1976. Currently a network of international routes is operated from Buenos Aires to five cities in Europe, to Los Angeles, Miami, New York and Montreal in North America, to 12 cities in South and Central America, and to Hong Kong, Auckland and Cape Town. For its domestic and regional services the airline uses Fokker F.28s, Boeing 737s and 727s, and for its long-haul flights Boeing 747s.

Fleet:
Boeing 707
Boeing 727
Boeing 737
Boeing 747
Fokker F.28

Aerolineas Argentinas operates the Boeing 747 as its primary type on long-haul routes. Principal destinations are Los Angeles, New York, London and Madrid.

Aeromexico

Established on 1 September 1934 as Aeronaves de Mexico, Aeromexico adopted its current title in February 1972. The airline's first route was from Mexico City to Acapulco. After taking over many airlines in the 1950s, Aeromexico was taken over by the Mexican government in July 1959. The company's first international route, from Mexico City to New York, was flown in December 1957 by a Bristol Britannia from Mexico City to New York. The first Douglas DC-10 was handed over in April 1974. An extensive 31-point domestic network is served mainly with Douglas DC-9s, whereas on most international routes the DC-10s are flown, to such places as Panama City, Caracas, Bogota, Lima, Los Angeles, Tucson, Houston, Miami, New York, Madrid and Paris.

Fleet:
Douglas DC-8
Douglas DC-9
Douglas DC-10

Aero Peru

Established by the Peruvian government on 22 May 1973 as the country's national carrier, Aero Peru replaced Aerlineas Peruanas SA(APSA) and the military-controlled SATCO. The new airline's initial equipment for use on the domestic services were three ex-SATCO Fokker F.28 Fellowships. International services, with two leased VIASA Douglas DC-8-50s, commenced on 29 July 1974 with flights to Santiago and Buenos Aires. Briefly (from December 1978 to 1982) Aero Peru operated two Lockheed L-1011 TriStar 1s. Aero Peru became a private company on 24 July 1981.

Currently the airline operates Douglas DC-8-62s and Boeing 727s to many destinations in South America, plus Mexico City and Panama City, and on its domestic services it uses mainly Fokker F.27s and F.28s.

Fleet:
Boeing 727
Douglas DC-8

Fokker F.27
Fokker F.28

Air Afrique

Formed on 28 March 1961 by UAT and Air France in conjunction with 11 newly-independent French colonies, Air Afrique started domestic flights with Douglas DC-4s and DC-6s in June 1961, and international services on 16 October 1961 between Paris and the African states with leased Lockheed Super Constellations. Jet services with Douglas DC-8s started on 5 June 1962. Since Air Afrique's conception two airlines, Air Gabon and Cameroon Airlines, have withdrawn from the consortium, but before this happened Togo joined in 1965. The airline's first wide-bodied aircraft was a

Douglas DC-10-30 delivered on 29 February 1973. Currently Air Afrique operates internal services to 22 African states, and services to Bordeaux, Paris, Nice, Geneva, Zurich, Rome, Las Palmas, New York and Jeddah.

Fleet:
Airbus A300
Boeing 727

Boeing 747
Douglas DC-8
Douglas DC-10

The Ivory Coast's national carrier, Air Afrique, uses Airbus A300Bs on services to Europe and the Middle East.

Air Algérie

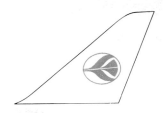

Established in 1947 as the Compagnie Générale de Transports Aériens, the current Air Algérie was formed in 1953 when CGTA took over Compagnie Air Transport. The airline's first pure-jet aircraft was the Sud-Aviation Caravelle, which entered service on 12 January 1960 between Algiers and Paris. The Caravelles were replaced on the international routes by the Boeing 727 and 737 which were handed over during 1971. In 1972 the Algerian government took over the airline. Air Algérie first used a wide-bodied aircraft on 25 November 1974 when it leased its first Airbus A300.

Scheduled passenger and cargo flights are flown to North and West Africa, the Middle East and 13 points in Europe. Domestic flights are now operated by a separate division of Air Algérie known as Inter Air Services, which was formed in 1984.

Fleet:

Airbus A300
Airbus A310
Boeing 727

Boeing 737
Fokker F.27
Lockheed L-100-30

Boeing 727s and 737s (illustrated) are used by Air Algérie throughout Europe, North Africa and the Middle East.

AirCal

Formed in 1966 as Air California, the airline began operations on 16 January 1967 with Lockheed L-188 Electras from Orange County Airport (south of Los Angeles). Within two years the airline had expanded sufficiently to enable Air California to purchase Boeing 737s, of which the first entered service on 27 October 1968. In April 1981 the present title was adopted together with a completely new colour scheme. AirCal operates a high-frequency one-class interstate network from Orange County Airport to numerous points along the Pacific coastline from Seattle in the north to San José in the south. Charter work within the USA is also undertaken. The other type currently operated is the

Douglas DC-9-80, the first of this latest variant being delivered in October 1981.

Fleet:
Boeing 737
Douglas DC-9-80

Air Canada

The Canadian state airline was formed on 10 April 1937 as Trans Canada Airlines. The airline's first aircraft was a Lockheed L-10A Electra which inaugurated its first survey flights on 7 July from Vancouver to Seattle. Multi-stop transcontinental passenger services were started on 1 April 1939 from Seattle and Vancouver to Toronto, Ottawa and Montreal. On 22 July 1943 transatlantic services (to London via Reykjavik) using modified Avro Lancasters were started. On 1 April 1955 TCA became the first airline in the Americas to operate the Vickers Viscount. Five years later, on 1 April 1960, the first pure-jet services started with a Douglas DC-8-43 on the Montreal–Toronto–Vancouver route. The title Air Canada was adopted in 1964, together with what is basically the current colour scheme. At present 23,500 staff are employed, the majority of them at Toronto and at the air-

line's head office in Montreal. The first wide-bodied aircraft (a Boeing 747-133) was delivered on 11 February 1971. With the Lockheed L-1011 TriStars and Boeing 767-233s the airline operates high-density and long-haul routes to Europe, the Far East, the Caribbean and North America. On its short/medium-haul routes the airline uses mainly Douglas DC-9s and Boeing 727s. In addition to scheduled passenger work the airline operates scheduled cargo and charter flights throughout the world.

Fleet:

Boeing 727
Boeing 747
Boeing 767

Douglas DC-8
Douglas DC-9
Lockheed L-1011 TriStar

Air Canada has bought the Boeing 767 for operation on high density routes throughout Canada and the United States.

Air Charter International

Formed on 7 February 1966 as a wholly-owned subsidiary of Air France to operate charter and inclusive tour flights, Air Charter International began operations in July 1966. The airline's original equipment comprised Sud-Aviation Caravelles transferred from Air France. Since that time ACI has introduced the Boeing 727 (in May 1972) and larger equipment is leased on an ad hoc

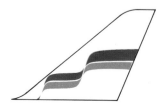

Air Charter International (continued)

basis from the parent company and other French independent airlines. Currently the airline is owned 80 per cent by Air France and 20 per cent by Air Inter.

Fleet:
Boeing 727

Sud-Aviation Caravelle

Air Europe

Air Europe operated its first flight with a Boeing 737-2S3 on 4 May 1979 after the airline was formed as an associate member of the Intasun Group on 18 July 1978. The airline's headquarters is at London (Gatwick) airport. On 6 April 1983 the airline took delivery of its first Boeing 757-236, which operates with Boeing 737s on charter and inclusive tour flights from numerous regional airports to points throughout Europe and to North Africa.

Fleet:
Boeing 737

Boeing 757

Air Europe provides inclusive tours and charter flights from London-Gatwick and other regional airports with Boeing 737s and 757s.

Air France

Formed on 30 August 1933 by the merger of four airlines (Air Orient, Air Union, CIDNA and SGTA) Air France emerged with 259 aircraft of 35 different types. On 1 January 1946 all French transport was nationalized, and the Société Nationale Air France was set up on 16 June 1948. On 26 August 1953 the airline operated its first pure-jet service with a de Havilland Comet 1 from Paris to

Air France (continued)

Beirut via Rome, followed on 15 September 1953 by its first service with the turboprop-powered Vickers Viscount 708 on the Paris to London route. On 21 January 1976 the Western world's first services by supersonic airliner took place when Air France and British Airways inaugurated Concorde operations simultaneously, Air France flying from Paris via Dakar to Rio de Janeiro. The airline's main base is at Paris Charles de Gaulle airport, and worldwide the airline employs just over 34,500 staff. For long-haul flights Air France operates mainly the Boeing 747 (the first was delivered on 20 March 1970) and, on limited services, the Concorde. For its short medium-haul routes

Boeing 727 and 737 plus Airbus A300 and A310 are operated. The world's first A300 service was flown by Air France between Paris and London on 23 May 1974. Currently the airline operates 19 A300s and will shortly have five A310s in service, whilst on order are 25 A320s which should be delivered towards the end of the 1980s. Air France also operates the Postale de Nuit internal mail service with Fokker F.27 Mk 500s and the world's only civil Transalls. Air France has a financial interest in the following airlines: Air Charter International, Air Gabon, Air Guadeloupe, Air Djibouti, Air Inter, Air Madagasgar, Air Mauritius, Cameroon Airlines, Middle East Airlines, Royal Air Maroc and Tunis Air.

Fleet:
Aérospatiale/BAe
Concorde
Airbus A300
Airbus A310

Boeing 727
Boeing 737
Boeing 747
Fokker F.27
Transall C.160

Air Gabon

Air services by the Compagnie Aérienne Gabonaise began in 1951 with Beech and de Havilland aircraft on local services from the airline's base at Libreville. In July 1968 the airline became Gabon's national carrier under the name Société Nationale Transgabon, the current airline name being adopted in 1974. In May 1977 Air Gabon withdrew from the Air Afrique consortium and began its own services. For the regional routes two Fokker F.28 Mk 2000s were delivered in July 1974, together with a Boeing 737. For the long-haul routes to Europe the airline uses its lone Boeing 747-2Q2B, of which it took delivery on 5 October 1978.

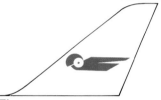

Fleet:
Boeing 737
Boeing 747
Fokker F.28
Vickers Vanguard

Air Gabon utilizes two Fokker F.28s on its regional routes, where the type's low running cost and short-field performance make it ideal.

Air France operated the West's first supersonic service with the Aérospatiale/British Aerospace Concorde, flying from Paris–Charles de Gaulle to Rio de Janeiro, via Dakar, on 21 January 1976.

Air India

Formed in July 1932 by Neville Vintcent and J. R. D. Tata, the airline which later became Air India made its first flight with a de Havilland Moth on 15 October, between Karachi and Madras. On 29 July 1946 the airline changed its name from Tata Air Line to Air India. On 8 March 1948 the title Air India International was adopted and with a Lockheed L-749 Constellation the airline started flights to London via Cairo and Geneva, three months after the title Air India International had been adopted. On 1 August 1953 the airline was nationalized. The first jet, a Boeing 707-437, was delivered on 18 February 1960 and entered service on 19 April between India and the UK. On 8 June 1962 the airline reverted to the name of Air India. Air India's first Boeing 747-237B was delivered on 22 March 1971 and entered service to London on 21 May 1971. With four Airbus A300s the airline operates the

majority of its passenger flights from Bombay, Delhi, Trivondrum, Madras and Amritsar to cities in the Far and Middle East, Europe, Africa, Australia and North America. For the airline's all-freight services Air India operates leased Douglas DC-8-63s.

Fleet:
Airbus A300
Boeing 747
Douglas DC-8-63

Air India is mainly concerned with international flights from India's main cities. The Boeing 747 forms the most important part of the fleet.

Air Inter

Lignes Aériennes Intérieures, more commonly known as Air Inter, was formed in late 1954 to operate French domestic flights. On 17 March 1958 the airline operated its first service from Paris to Strasbourg, but all services were suspended in November 1958 due to non-realization of financial targets. The airline restarted on 1 July 1960 with various marks of Lockheed Constellation, Vickers Viscount, Douglas DC-3 and Sud-Aviation Caravelle leased

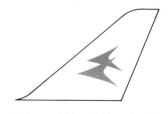

from Air France, Vickers Vikings leased from Airnautic and Douglas DC-6Bs leased from TAI. During 1962 six Viscount 708s

Air Inter (continued)

were bought from Air France, and in 1965 three Caravelles were ordered by Air France for the internal airline. On 16 May 1974 Air Inter took delivery of its first Dassault Mercure, and was the only airline to operate this 150-seat twin-jet. The airline's first and at present only wide-bodied aircraft is the Airbus A300, of which the first was delivered on 28 September 1976. Together with Caravelles and Fokker F.27s, Air Inter operates an extensive network of passenger and cargo flights from Paris to most of the major cities in France. Air France and French Railways each own 25 per cent, 15 per cent is held by UTA and the balance is held by various French interests.

Fleet:
Airbus A300
Dassault Mercure
Fokker F.27
Sud-Aviation Caravelle

Air Jamaica

Formed in 1968 by the Jamaican government (60 per cent) and Air Canada (40 per cent), Air Jamaica began operations on 1 April 1969 with two leased Air Canada Douglas DC-9-32s and a Douglas DC-8. The DC-9s operated to Miami and the DC-8 to New York. On 1 April 1974 Air Jamaica operated its first service to London with a DC-8; this service ceased on 1 April 1981, but is currently operated jointly with British Airways. The latest addition to the fleet are two Airbus A300s which arrived in Jamaica in February 1983 and operated their first service from Kingston to Toronto on 27 February. Currently the airline operates two types, the Boeing 727 on the Caribbean and southern US services, and the A300s

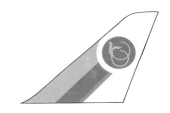

mainly on the long-distance routes to New York, Philadelphia, Chicago and Toronto.

Fleet:
Airbus A300
Boeing 727

Air Lanka

Air Lanka was formed on 10 January 1979 to take over from Air Ceylon, which had ceased trading on 31 March 1978. The airline's first services were operated with two leased Singapore Airlines Boeing 707s. Regional services began in April 1980 with a leased Boeing 737. The Lockheed L-1011 TriStar operated its first service from Colombo to Paris (Orly) on 2 November 1980. For use on the long-haul high-density routes such as that from Colombo to London (Gatwick) Air Lanka has leased a Boeing 747-238B, but the majority of the airline's services are operated by L-1011s. Currently Air Lanka operates to 16 cities in

Asia, and to Amsterdam, Frankfurt, London, Vienna and Zurich in Europe. At present the Sri Lankan government has 60 per cent interest, the balance being held by public companies in Sri Lanka.

Fleet:
Boeing 737

Boeing 747
Lockheed L-1011 TriStar

Air Malta

Although the origins of Air Malta can be traced back to the late 1940s, the current airline was established on 26 March 1973 and began independent scheduled services between Malta and London on 1 April 1973 with a leased Pakistan International Airlines Boeing 720. Currently the airline operates three Boeing 737s (purchased new in 1978) and Boeing 720s on its flights from Luqa Airport in Malta to 11 cities in Europe, and to Cairo, Tripoli, Kuwait and Damascus.

Fleet:
Boeing 720
Boeing 737

Air Malta flies the Boeing 737 and Boeing 720 from its base at Luqa to several destinations in Europe and the Middle East.

Air Mauritius

Although Air Mauritius was founded on 14 June 1967, the airline did not start operations until 1972 using Piper Navajos on inter-island services. International services were at first carried out by the founder shareholding airlines, namely British Airways, Air India and Air France, but on 1 January 1977 Air Mauritius began international services with a leased British Airways Boeing 707. The latest (and a major) step for the airline was the acquisition, on lease from South African Airways, of a Boeing 747SP. This long-range wide-body airliner operated its first flight, to London, on 3 November 1984. Currently the airline

operates two de Havilland Canada DHC-6 Twin Otters on inter-island services, and on its international routes it uses two Boeing 707s and the single Boeing 747SP to destinations in Africa and Europe, as well as a service to Bombay.

Fleet:
Boeing 707

Boeing 747SP
de Havilland Canada DHC-6

Air New Zealand

In April 1940 the governments of New Zealand (50 per cent), Australia (30 per cent) and the United Kingdom (20 per cent) teamed to form Tasman Empire Airways Limited on 3 April 1940. With a Short S.30 flying-boat services were operated between Auckland and Sydney. In May 1954 the UK government relinquished its interest to the Australians, and on 14 May the airline's first landplane (a Douglas DC-6) was flown from Christchurch to Melbourne. On 1 April 1965 the airline became known as Air New Zealand, and on 3 October 1965 the first jet service (with a DC-8-52) was flown between Christchurch and Sydney, followed on 14 December by the first service between Auckland and Los Angeles. On 7 February 1973 the first Douglas DC-10-30 service was operated. These wide-bodied aircraft remained in service until 1981, when they were replaced on long-haul flights by the Boeing 747-219B. On 1 April 1978 the domestic airline New Zealand National Airways Corporation merged with Air New Zealand, and at present Fokker F.27s and Boeing 737s operate the airline's domestic and regional services. In the near future Boeing 767-219s will start operating within Australasia, leaving the Boeing 747s on the high-density and long-haul routes. Airlines in which Air New Zealand has an interest are Safe Air (100 per cent), Polynesian Airlines (10 per cent) and Mount Cook Airlines (11.9 per cent).

Fleet:
Boeing 737
Boeing 747
Fokker F.27

Air New Zealand provides a comprehensive service throughout the two home islands with the Fokker F.27 and the Boeing 737 (illustrated).

Air UK

One of the United Kingdom's youngest airlines was formed on 1 January 1980 when British Island Airways, Air Anglia, Air Wales and Air West merged to form Air UK. These four airlines had been operating domestic and regional services, in BIA's case since November 1962. Air UK is the UK's third-largest scheduled service airline, and currently operates Fokker F.27s and F.28s, Handley Page Heralds, Shorts 330s and 360s on scheduled passenger and cargo flights, plus charters, between 20 airports

Air UK (continued)

in the UK, and international services to Amsterdam, Bergen, Dublin, Stavanger and Paris in Europe. The airline's main engineering bases are at Norwich and Exeter, where contracted airline work is also performed.

Fleet:
Fokker F.27
Fokker F.28
Handley Page Herald
Shorts 330
Shorts 360

Air Wisconsin

Operations as a scheduled commuter airline by Air Wisconsin began on 23 August 1965 to points in the state of Wisconsin. Since that time Air Wisconsin has grown into a regional carrier serving the states of Illinois, Indiana, Michigan, Minnesota, Ohio and Wisconsin with a fleet of de Havilland Canada DHC-7s. The airline's first jet type is the British Aerospace 146-200, of which the first was handed over on 10 June 1983.

Fleet:
British Aerospace 146
de Havilland Canada DHC-7

Air Zaïre

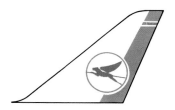

What is now Air Zaïre was formed on 28 June 1961 as Air Congo with assistance from SABENA, and initial services were carried out with Douglas DC-4s and DC-6s. Air Congo's first jet service was in 1963 between Kinshasa and Brussels, using a leased SABENA Boeing 707. When the Congo republic changed its name to Zaïre, Air Congo was renamed Air Zaïre in October 1971. Air Zaïre is owned 80 per cent by the Zaïre government, and the balance is held by local concerns. At present Pan American gives the airline technical assistance. Air Zaïre operates passenger and cargo services to domestic points from Kinshasa and Luhambashi, and international services to Abidjan Bujumbura, Conakry, Dakar, Douala, Lagos, Libreville, Lome, Luanda and Nairobi in Africa, and to Athens,

Brussels, Paris and Rome in Europe. Fokker F.27 and Boeing 737 are used for domestic and regional services, while the Douglas DC-10 and Douglas DC-8 are operated on long-distance flights.

Fleet:
Boeing 737
Douglas DC-8
Douglas DC-10
Fokker F.27

Air Zimbabwe

Until the disbandment of the Central African Airways Corporation in 1967, Air Rhodesia (as it was then known) had been a wholly-owned subsidiary of CAAC from 1964. But from 1967 and using firstly Vickers Viscounts and Douglas DC-3s, the airline began operating independently. Air Rhodesia acquired three Boeing 720s for

Air Zimbabwe (continued)

domestic and regional services. In June 1979 the airline adopted the current title upon its country's independence. In July 1983 Air Zimbabwe took over Affretair. Currently scheduled passenger and cargo services link Harare with eight points

domestically, and internationally the airline flies to Blantyre, Durban, Gabarone, Johannesburg, Lusaka and Nairobi in Africa, and to Athens, Frankfurt and London in Europe. Services to Perth and Sydney are operated in conjunction with Qantas.

Fleet:
Boeing 707
Boeing 720

Vickers Viscount

Alaska Airlines

Operations by this Alaskan airline began in 1930 as Star Air Services, mainly with single-engined types. In 1937 the airline modified its name to Star Air Lines, and adopted its current title on 1 November 1943. In 1951 Alaska Airlines began flying to the US mainland. In the early 1960s Convair CV-340s were used on intra-state services, and Douglas DC-6As on flights to Seattle and on charters. The airline's first jet was the Convair CV-880, which entered service on 20 August 1961. The Convair CV-880s were replaced five years later by Boeing 727s, and at present with the Boeing 737 Alaska Airlines operates

scheduled passenger and cargo services within Alaska and to the states of California, Oregon and Washington.

Fleet:
Boeing 727
Boeing 737

Alaska Airlines serves destinations in Alaska and connects the state to the rest of the US. Boeing 727s and 737s are flown.

Alia

Formed in October 1963, the Jordanian state airline Alia began operation 15 Deceber 1963 with two leased Douglas DC-7s and two Handley Page Heralds after taking over from Jordan Airways, which had ceased trading on 1 September 1960. The first jet to be used was a Sud-Aviation Caravelle 10R, of which the first was delivered on 28 July 1965. With the Caravelle Alia was able to expand its network to include Paris and Rome. To help expand the network further during the 1970s Alia purchased the Boeing 747, the first being delivered on 13 April 1977, and this enabled the airline's Boeing 707s and 720s to be placed on lower-density passenger routes.

Assisting the Boeing 747s on the busier long-distance services is the Lockheed L-1011 TriStar, which entered service in late 1981. At present Alia flies to most capitals in the Middle and Far East, to destinations in Europe and Africa, and to New York. Subsidiaries include Arab Wings, Arab Air Services and Arab Air Cargo.

Fleet:
Boeing 707
Boeing 727

Boeing 747
Lockheed L-1011 TriStar

Alia's long range services are handled by the Lockheed L-1011 TriStar 500 (illustrated) and the Boeing 747-2D3B.

Alitalia

The Italian airline Aerolinee Italiane Internationale (known in short as Alitalia) was formed on 16 Septemer 1946 by the Italian government (47.5 per cent) and British European Airways (40 per cent), with private concerns holding the balance. On 1 September 1957 Alitalia and Linee Aeree Italiane SpA merged, when the name Alitalia was adopted officially. In April 1961 BEA relinquished all its interest. Domestic services began on 5 May 1947 and later in the year international services began to Cairo, Tripoli and Lisbon. The airline's original equipment was Fiat G.12s, Savoia-Marchetti S.M.95s and Avro Lancastrians. The first Douglas DC-8 was delivered to the

airline on 28 April 1960, followed on the next day by its first Caravelle, the latter entering service between Rome and London on 22 May 1960. The airline's first wide-bodied aircraft (a Boeing 747-143) was delivered on 13 May 1970. Subsidiary airlines are ATI and Aermediterranea. A major replanning of short-haul aircraft took

Alitalia (continued)

place in 1984, when the first of 30 Douglas DC-9-82s was delivered to replace the Boeing 727s, and with Airbus A300s these now operate the airline's European and Mediterranean networks. The long-haul routes to Africa, North and South America, the Middle and Far East, and Australia are operated by Boeing 747s.

Fleet:
Airbus A300

Boeing 747
Douglas DC-9

Europe and North Africa are served by Alitalia's Airbus A300 fleet, whilst the Boeing 747 takes care of the longer sectors.

All Nippon Airways

Formed in December 1952 as Japan Heli-copter and Aeroplane Transport Co. Limited, JHAT merged in March 1958 with Far East Airlines to form the current All Nippon Airways. On 23 June 1961 the air-line's first Vickers Viscount was delivered to replace the Convair CV-340/440 series. The airline operated its first pure jet, a

Operating a large network throughout the Japanese islands, All Nippon employs the Boeing 727 for medium-haul routes.

All Nippon Airways (continued)

leased Boeing 727, in April 1964. The first wide-bodied type ANA operated was the Lockheed L-1011 TriStar, which entered service in December 1973. Currently two other types of wide-bodied aircraft are used, namely the Boeing 747 and 767. All Nippon Airways is one of the world fastest-growing domestic airlines, and now operates just over 100 aircraft, of which nearly half are wide-bodied high-capacity types. The airline operates to 33 points in Japan with Boeing 727s, 737s, 747s and 767s plus Lockheed L-1011 TriStars and NAMC YS-11As. Additionally, charter services are flown to Hong Kong, Manila, Singapore and Beijing.

Fleet:
Boeing 727
Boeing 737
Boeing 747

Boeing 767
Lockheed L-1011 TriStar
NAMC YS-11A

Alyemda

The South Yemen (formerly Aden) state airline Alyemda was formed by presidential decree on 11 March 1971, and the airline started operations with Douglas DC-3s and DC-6s. The airline's first jet aircraft was a Boeing 720 delivered on 25 November 1974. Scheduled passenger and cargo services are operated from Aden to Abu Dhabi, Addis Ababa, Al Ghaydah, Ataq, Beihan, Damascus, Djibouti, Jeddah, Kuwait, Mogadishu, Qishu, Riyan Seiyun, Sharjah and Socotra.

Fleet:
Boeing 707
Boeing 720
de Havilland Canada DHC-7

Douglas DC-3
Douglas DC-6
Tupolev Tu-154

American Airlines

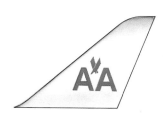

Formed on 11 April 1934 by taking over the interests of the Aviation Corporation which had been formed on 25 January 1930, American Airlines was one of the sponsors of the Western world's most successful aircraft, the Douglas DC-3, and by the time the USA had entered World War II in 1941 74 examples were being operated. Regular troop flights across the Atlantic were started on 20 June 1942, and were extended to India in 1943. American Airlines' first (and only) turboprop airliner was the Lockheed L-188 Electra, which entered service on 23 January 1959. During American Airlines' history it has sponsored the development of six aircraft, namely the Douglas DC-3, DC-7 and DC-10, the Convairs CV-240 and CV-990, and the Lockheed L-188 Electra. Its first pure jet was the Boeing 707-123, of which American Airlines was the first US domestic carrier to acquire and operate this aircraft, on 25 January 1959 between New York and Los Angeles. The first wide-bodied aircraft (a leased Pan American Boeing 747) entered service on 2 March 1970. Currently American Airlines operates a large fleet of aircraft throughout the USA, and also flies international services to Toronto and Montreal in the north

American Airlines operates a large network throughout the United States and several international routes. The newest type in service is the Boeing 767.

and to Mexico City, Acapulco and Guadalajara in the south, as well as numerous points in the Caribbean and from Dallas to London.

Fleet:

Boeing 727	Boeing 767
Boeing 747	Douglas DC-9
	Douglas DC-10

Ansett Airlines

The current Ansett Airlines was formed on 4 October 1957 when Ansett Airways took over National Airways to establish Ansett-ANA. The origins of both airlines can be traced back to 1936 and 1932 respectively. After the merger the airline ordered its first turboprop airliners, namely four Vickers Viscounts and three Lockheed Electras.

Ansett Airlines uses Boeing 727s on many domestic routes throughout Australia.

Ansett Airlines (continued)

The Boeing 727 entered service on 2 November 1964, and so became the airline's first pure jet. Until recently the Boeing 727 and Boeing 737 were the mainstay of the fleet, but on 4 May 1983 the first Boeing 767 was delivered, the first wide-bodied aircraft the airline had operated. Currently the main airline flies scheduled passenger and cargo flights throughout Australia. Four subsidiary airlines (New South Wales, Northern, South, and Western) operate Fokker F.27s and F.28s in their respective areas of Australia. The two major shareholders, holding 99 per cent of the stock, are Rupert Murdoch's News Corporation and Sir Peter Abeles Thomas with the Nationwide Transport Group.

Fleet:
Boeing 727
Boeing 737
Boeing 767
Fokker F.27
Fokker F.28

Ariana

Formed by the Afghan government (51 per cent) and the Indamer Company of India on 27 January 1955, Ariana began operations with four Douglas DC-3s provided by Indamer. In June 1956 Pan American acquired 49 per cent of the airline, and also offered assistance in expanding the airline's operations. On 25 March 1968 Ariana took delivery of its first Boeing 727 and later, on 21 September 1979 the airline's sole Douglas DC-10-30 was delivered. At present the airline's three aircraft link Kabul with Amritsar, Delhi, Tashkent, East Berlin,

Prague and Moscow. Charter flights are also undertaken.

Fleet:
Boeing 727
Douglas DC-10

Aero Trasporti Italiani

Aero Transporti Italiani (ATI) was formed on 13 December 1963 as a subsidiary of Alitalia to operate the parent company's domestic services previously carried out by Società Aerea Mediterranea. The new airline commenced operations on 3 June 1964 with Fokker F.27s, and in June 1966 using the F.27s started services to Libya on behalf of Libyan Arab Airlines. On 24 July 1969 the first Douglas DC-9 was delivered, and this now operates with the F.27s on an extensive domestic network linking the major cities of the Italian mainland and islands. In addition to airline work, ATI also has three F.27s that are used to calibrate

and check navaid systems. ATI also has a 45 per cent interest in Aeromediterranea.

Fleet:
Fokker F.27
Douglas DC-9

Austrian Airlines

Austrian Airlines was created by the merger on 30 September 1957 of Air Austria and Austrian Airways, neither of which had actually started operations. The airline took the name of its pre-war predecessor, which had been absorbed into Deutsche Luft-

Austrian Airlines (continued)

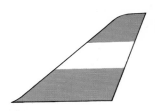

hansa in January 1939 and operated its first service was on 31 March 1958 between Vienna and London using a Vickers Viscount leased from Fred Olsen Air Transport. To cope with the proposed expansion of the airline the company ordered its first jet, the Sud-Aviation Caravelle. The first of these was delivered on 18 February 1963. On 10 June 1971 the first Douglas DC-9-32 was handed over, and this type progressively replaced the Caravelles. Since that time the airline has used various marks of the twin-jet, and at present operates only the DC-9. Scheduled passenger and cargo services from Vienna, Graz, Linz, Innsbruck, Klagenfurt and Salzburg are flown to 39 cities in Western and Eastern Europe, as well as to destinations in the Middle East. Through its subsidiary, Austrian Airtransport, charter flights are undertaken to points in Africa and Europe. In the near future two Airbus A310s will be accepted for use on the high-density routes.

Fleet:
Douglas DC-9

Austrian Airlines operates an all DC-9 fleet throughout Europe. Two Airbus A310s will shortly take over on high-density routes.

Aviaco

Formed on 18 February 1948 by a group of Bilbao businessmen, Aviaco was intended to operate all-cargo flights using Bristol Freighters. Scheduled passenger services were started in 1950 between Bilbao and Barcelona via Madrid, followed shortly afterwards by the airline's first international route to Marseilles. In 1960 Aviaco was leasing its first jets, namely Sud-Aviation Caravelles, from SABENA, and with these and other leased aircraft it started operating inclusive tours. Also in 1960 Iberia, the Spanish national airline, took a 66 per cent interest in the airline. Further Caravelles were transferred from Iberia, but have now been replaced by Douglas DC-9s. For use also on charter and inclusive tour work Douglas DC-8s have been transferred from the state airline. On Aviaco's scheduled operations DC-9s and Fokker F.27s are used, and shortly these are to be joined by Airtech CN-235s. The major shareholder,

27

Aviaco (continued)

with a 90 per cent interest, is a Spanish government agency, the Instituto Nacional de Industria, the same department that controls Iberia.

Fleet:
Douglas DC-8
Douglas DC-9
Fokker F.27

Avianca

Formed on 5 December 1919 as Sociedad Colombo-Alemana de Transportes Aereos by three German settlers and five Colombians, Avianca is thus the oldest airline in the Americas and the longest continuously running airline in the world. The first service, between Bogota and Baranquilla, took place in September 1921. In 1931 Pan American acquired an 80 per cent interest in SCADTA. In June 1940 SCADTA merged with Servicio Aereo Colombiano to form Aerovias Nacionales de Colombia SA (Avianca). During the 1940s the German airliners were replaced with Douglas DC-3s and DC-4s, as well as some Boeing 247s. On 4 January 1947 the airline operated its first service to Balboa, followed by one to Miami on 22 January 1947. Transatlantic services to Madrid and Hamburg were started in March 1950. Pending the delivery

of its own jets (Boeing 720s) Avianca leased Boeing 707s from Pan American, the first entering service on 17 October 1960. The next major equipment change was the introduction in November 1976 of the Boeing 747. In 1978 Avianca bought out the remaining Pan American interest. Currently the airline operates an extensive domestic and regional network with its Boeing 727s, whilst the long-haul international schedule to North and South America plus Europe is operated by Boeing 707s and 747s.

Fleet:
Boeing 707

Boeing 727
Boeing 747

Colombia's national airline Avianca still operates the Boeing 707. These are usually employed on long-haul routes to Europe and North America.

Aviogenex

Aviogenex was established on 21 May 1968 as Genex Airlines, the air transport division of the Yugoslav state-owned Generalexport organization. Operations commenced in April 1969 with two Tupolev Tu-134As. The airline concentrates on passenger charters and inclusive tour work throughout Europe, the Mediterranean and the Middle East with its fleet of Tu-134As and two Boeing 727s. All-freight flights are operated to North Africa, the Middle East and the Persian Gulf.

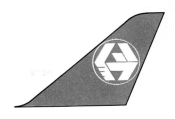

Fleet:
Boeing 727
Tupolev Tu-134

Aviogenex is unusual insofar as it operates a mixed American-Soviet fleet. This Tu-134 is employed alongside the Boeing 727 throughout Europe and North Africa.

Balair

Formed in 1953 as a flying school, Balair first flew charter flights in 1957 with Vickers Vikings. Initially Swissair had a 36 per cent interest in the airline, but this has now been increased to 57 per cent. In 1959 a Douglas DC-4 was acquired from Swissair, and was followed by a DC-6 in December 1961. The airline's first jet aircraft was a McDonnell Douglas DC-9 delivered on 17 April 1970. Balair's first wide-bodied aircraft was a McDonnell Douglas DC-10-30 handed over on 30 January 1979. Future plans include the acquisition of an Airbus A310 to join the fleet that currently operates passenger and cargo charters and inclusive tour work to

Europe, North Africa, the Americas, the Far East and West Africa.

Fleet:
Douglas DC-8
Douglas DC-9
Douglas DC-10

Balkan Bulgarian Airlines

Under the name of Bulgarshe Vazdusne Sobstenie a new airline started operations on 29 July 1947. This first airline was taken over in 1949 by a Bulgarian and Soviet undertaking who formed TABSO, which began services with Lisunov Li-2s (Soviet-

Balkan Bulgarian Airlines (continued)

built DC-3s) supplied by the USSR. In 1954 TABSO became totally owned by the Bulgarian government when the Soviets withdrew their 50 per cent interest. Since that time expansion has seen the introduction of Ilyushin Il-18s in 1962, Tupolev Tu-134s in 1968 and Tu-154s in the late 1970s. The current title was adopted in 1968 and the airline now operates to 44 cities in Europe, Asia and Africa, plus an eight-point domestic network. Balkan also operates an agricultural aviation service.

Antonov An-24
Ilyushin Il-18
Mil Mi-8
Tupolev Tu-134
Tupolev Tu-154
Yakovlev Yak-40

Fleet:
Antonov An-12

Bangladesh Biman

Bangladesh Biman was formed on 4 January 1972 as the national carrier of the new state of Bangladesh (formerly East Pakistan). Exactly one month later services began with leased Douglas DC-3s, which were replaced by Fokker F.27s in March. On 28 April 1972 the airline's first international service was operated, between Dacca and Calcutta. The airline's first service to London from Dacca was flown on 1 January 1973, using a leased Donaldson International Boeing 707-321. Further Boeing 707s and F.27s were added to the fleet and the route network in the East was accordingly enlarged. To assist the F.27s on the regional and domestic routes, two Fokker F.28 Fellowships were delivered in the autumn of 1981. August 1983 saw the arrival of the first two Douglas DC-10-30s, and these wide-bodied aircraft have now

replaced the Boeing 707s on the long-haul flights to Europe. At present Bangladesh Biman operates domestic services to six points, plus international services to numerous cities in Asia and to Amsterdam, Athens, London, and Rome in Europe.

Fleet:
Douglas DC-10-30
Fokker F.27
Fokker F.28

Bangladesh Biman flies two Douglas DC-10s on its long-haul flights. These replaced Boeing 707s in this role.

Braathens SAFE

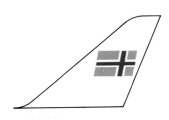

Formed by the Norwegian shipping owner Ludwig G. Braathens on 26 March 1946, Braathens South American And Far East Transport began charter operations in February 1947 with three Douglas DC-4s on services to South America and Hong Kong, and for five years from 1949 operated scheduled services to Hong Kong. In 1952 scheduled domestic services were inaugurated, initially with de Havilland Herons. On 20 December 1958 Braathens became the second operator to take delivery of the Fokker F.27 Friendship. In 1969 Boeing 737-205s and Fokker F.28s were delivered, and these eventually replaced the F.27s and Douglas DC-6Bs then in service. To expand the airline's charter business two Boeing 767-205s were delivered in 1984. Braathens currently operates scheduled passenger and cargo flights to 12 points in Norway, and charter flights are undertaken to Europe and North Africa.

Fleet:
Boeing 737
Boeing 767
Fokker F.28

Britannia Airways

Operations by an airline named Euravia commenced on 5 May 1962, a Lockheed Constellation flying a charter service from Manchester to Palma. Shortly after the introduction of the Bristol Britannia Euravia changed its name to Britannia Airways, the date being 16 August 1964. On 26 April 1965 the airline became a wholly-owned subsidiary of Thomson Holidays. The airline's first Boeing 737-204 was delivered on 7 July 1968. At one time in the early 1970s Britannia was operating Model 737s as far afield as Hong Kong, Bangkok and Kuala Lumpur. From 1973 until 1984 only Boeing 737s were operated, but as from 18 February 1984 Britannia Airways began to use its newly-delivered Boeing 767-204. Over 70 destinations are regularly served from the UK. In addition to flights from Luton, the airline operates charter and inclusive tour services from 20 other UK airfields. In 1983 in terms of passengers carried and passenger miles flown the airline was the largest independent operator in Europe.

Fleet:
Boeing 737
Boeing 767

Britannia owns a large fleet of Boeing 737s for use on its holiday and charter routes. These are supplemented by the Boeing 767.

British Air Ferries

British United Air Ferries was formed in January 1963 by the merger of Channel Air Bridge (founded in 1959) and Silver City Airways (founded in 1948). In September 1967 the present name was adopted. In October 1971 the airline was taken over by T. D. Keegan from Air Holdings Limited. Scheduled vehicle ferry flights were at that time being carried out by Aviation Trader Carvairs on services from Southend to Le Touquet, Ostend, Rotterdam and Basle. In 1983 the airline was split up, and the air transport division was bought by Jadepoint. BAF now operates scheduled passenger services linking Southend with Basle and Ostend, and cargo work is also undertaken.

Fleet:
Handley Page Herald
Vickers Viscount

British Airtours

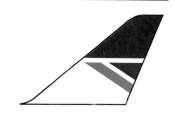

Formed as a charter and inclusive tour subsidiary of BEA on 24 April 1969, BEA Airtours operations began with de Havilland Comet 4Bs on 5 March 1970. In December 1971 the first ex-BOAC Boeing 707 was delivered, and this type eventually replaced the Comets. With the Boeings the carrier expanded its network to include transatlantic charters. The present name, British Airtours, was adopted in 1974 when the parent company became known as British Airways. Since that time the airline has replaced its Boeing 707s with Boeing 737s and Lockheed L-1011 TriStars, and these operate inclusive tour and charter flights on behalf of the company.

Fleet:
Boeing 737
Lockheed L-1011 TriStar

British Airways

The origins of British Airways can be traced back to 31 March 1924, when four pioneering airlines merged to form Imperial Airways. In 1935 a pre-war British Airways was formed by the union of three small airlines which, unlike Imperial Airways, concentrated their services on Europe. On 24 November 1939 the two airlines were merged by an act of parliament to form BOAC. A new European division (BEA) was formed in August 1946. In July and August 1950 BEA used the world's first turboprop airliner, the Vickers Viscount 630, on experimental flights from London to Paris and Edinburgh, and in May 1952 BOAC started the world's first pure jet services from London to Johannesburg with the de Havilland Comet 1. British Airways Helicopters was formed in 1964 to operate services from Penzance to Isles of Scilly, and to undertake related work and air/sea rescue operations. In early 1969 BEA formed a new charter and inclusive tour division, namely BEA Airtours (now named British Airtours). On 31 October 1970 BEA completed its takeover of Cambrian Airways and BKS/Northeast to form a regional division. The first Boeing 747-136 was delivered to BOAC on 22 April 1970 and entered service one year later on the North Atlantic routes. On 1 September 1972 BOAC and BEA joined to form British Airways, although the two airlines did not take up their new identity fully until 1 April 1974. British

Flying from London's Heathrow airport, British Airways operates a massive network throughout the world. Lower density European routes are flown by the Boeing 737.

British Airways (continued)

Airways and Air France operated the Western world's first supersonic airliner on 21 January 1976, BA flying an Aérospatiale/BAe Concorde between London and Bahrain. Currently British Airways' European services are being modernized by the introduction of further Boeing 737s and 757s, which are replacing the Hawker Siddeley Tridents which have been in service since the 1960s. On 4 December 1984 the airline's new colour scheme and corporate image was revealed, this being a prelude to the airline's denationalization during 1985. British Airways' route network is the largest in the world, and at present serves 120 cities in 65 countries. The airline operates to all the continents excluding South America, but from April 1985 all the continents of the world will be served.

Fleet:
Aérospatiale/BAe Concorde
BAC One-Eleven
Boeing 737
Boeing 747
Boeing 757
Hawker Siddeley HS.748
Hawker Siddeley Trident
Lockheed L-1011 TriStar

British Caledonian Airways

The history of British Caledonian Airways dates back to 27 April 1961, when Caledonian Airways was officially formed. Operations with a leased SABENA Douglas DC-7C began on 29 November 1961, the first service being a charter flight from London to Barbados. By 1967 the Bristol Britannia had taken over the duties of the DC-7Cs. On 13 July 1967 the airline's first pure jet (a Boeing 707) was leased. On 30 November 1970 Caledonian Airways took over British United Airways, and initially the combined airline was known as Caledonian/BUA. This amalgamation meant that for the first time scheduled services were operated. On 31 March 1971 the airline was awarded the old BOAC routes from London to Lagos, Kano and Accra, Tripoli being added in July. In September

1971 the airline adopted its current name and colour scheme. Following a further government review in 1976 the airline was given an additional route to Africa and the South American services that British Airways had been operating (the latter is to be reversed in April 1985). A major step for the airline was acquisition on 31 March 1977 of its first wide-bodied aircraft (the Douglas DC-10-30), and this aircraft has now re-

The mainstay of British Caledonian's long-haul scheduled services is the Douglas DC-10 Series 30, which has replaced the Boeing 707.

British Caledonian Airways (continued)

placed the Boeing 707 on the airline's long-haul routes. On its short-haul and domestic routes the airline operates the BAC One-Eleven and Airbus A310s. Subsidiary airlines of BCAL are British Caledonian Helicopters, formed in 1979 to operate in the North Sea; British Caledonian Commuters, formed in 1982 to offer commuter airline feeder links into the BCAL network; and

BCAL Charter, which operates charter services with Douglas DC-10-10s.

Fleet:
Airbus A310
BAC One-Eleven
Boeing 747
Douglas DC-10

British Midland Airways

On 16 February 1949 Derby Aviation (BMA's originator) was registered as an airline, and initially operated the de Havilland D.H.89As. The earliest trace of the airline is October 1938, when a reserve training school was formed at Burnaston and named Air Schools. In April 1955 the first Douglas DC-3 was purchased by the airline and by 1958 three DC-3s were being operated on charter and scheduled work originating from Derby. On 12 March 1959 the airline changed its name to Derby Airways, this being followed on 1 October 1964 by a further change to British Midland Airways. On 1 February 1965 the airline bought its first turboprop airliner, a Handley Page Herald, and in April the same year moved to its current base at Castle Donington. The airline's first scheduled service to London (Heathrow) was from Teesside in 1969. The airline's first jet, a BAC One-Eleven 523FJ, was delivered on 17 February 1970, and

BMA's first of many Boeing 707s was delivered in the April. Until 1974 the aircraft were used for inclusive tour work, but from that time the airline went into the leasing business with its Model 707s, a function they carried out until October 1984 when they were withdrawn from use. Currently the airline operates scheduled domestic services from numerous regional airports, plus international services to Amsterdam, Brussels and Paris. BMA also flies charter services, mainly to the Mediterranean countries. BMA holds a majority interest in two airlines, namely Manx Airlines and Loganair.

Fleet:
Douglas DC-9
Fokker F.27

Shorts 360
Vickers Viscount

BWIA International

British West Indian Airways was formed on 27 November 1939 by a New Zealander, Lovell Yerex, and operations with a Lockheed L-18 Lodestar started in November 1940. By 1947 Yerex had sold his interest to the Trinidad government, the balance being held by British interests. On 28 July 1955 the first Vickers Viscount to be operated in the Caribbean was delivered for local services. Using Bristol Britannias leased from BOAC, transatlantic services were started on 29 April 1960 between Trinidad and London via Barbados and New York. The Viscounts were replaced in 1964-5 after the

delivery of the airline's first jet aircraft, a Boeing 727. Further improvements to the long-haul routes came in 1966 when Boeing 720s were introduced into the network. The airline's first (and currently only) wide-bodied aircraft is the Lockheed L-1011 TriStar, which entered service in

BWIA International (continued)

January 1980, replacing the Boeing 707s. Also in January 1980 Trinidad and Tobago (BWIA International) Airways was formed by the merger of BWIA International with the government-owned TTAS. This merger means that the joint airline now operates scheduled passenger and cargo flights to 11 points in the Caribbean, plus services to Miami, New York and London.

Fleet:
Douglas DC-9
Hawker Siddeley HS.748
Lockheed L-1011 TriStar

Brymon Airways

Brymon Airways started regional services in June 1972, and the airline currently operates from Plymouth and Newquay to numerous points in Great Britain, the Channel Islands, France and Eire. Oil-related services are flown from the airline's Scottish base at Aberdeen. Currently the airline is proposing to start STOL inter-city services from the London dockland to points in the UK and Europe using the de Havilland Canada DHC-7 and DHC-8, which are still to be delivered.

Fleet:
de Havilland Canada DHC-6
de Havilland Canada DHC-7
de Havilland Canada DHC-8

CAAC

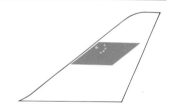

The origins of the People's Republic of China airline CAAC can be traced to a Sino-Soviet airline which was formed in 1939 to operate services between China and the central USSR. Between 1939 and 1954 numerous airlines operated in China, but the current airline was established in 1954 by the Chinese government. Initially the airline used Lisunov Li-2s, which were followed by Ilyushin Il-14s and in 1960 by the turboprop Il-18. To replace its ageing Soviet types CAAC purchased Hawker Siddeley Tridents, first from PIA in 1970 and then new from the manufacturers in 1972. The long-haul services from 1973 were served by the Il-62 and Boeing 707. With the Model 707 services from Peking to Tokyo started in August 1974. The airline's only wide-bodied aircraft, Boeing 747SPs, were delivered from February 1980, and work alongside the Boeing 707s and Il-62 on long-haul and high-density routes. Currently CAAC operates passenger and cargo services to 17 countries in Asia, Africa, Europe and North America, plus an extensive domestic network that has 171 services linking 29 provinces of the country. The airline also carries out non-airline work such as pest control, crop spraying and air surveys.

Fleet:
Antonov An-24
Boeing 707
Boeing 737
Boeing 747
Douglas DC-9

Hawker Siddeley Trident
Ilyushin Il-14
Ilyushin Il-18
Ilyushin Il-62
Lisunov Li-2

Cameroon Airlines

Cameroon Airlines was formed on 26 July 1971 when the government withdrew the airline from the Air Afrique consortium. Technical assistance was initially provided

Working mainly on long-range routes to the United States and European cities, the Boeing 747SP is Communist China's only wide-body jet.

Cameroon Airlines (continued)

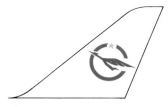

by Air France, which also leased the new airline a Boeing 707 to start operations. Regional services are carried out by Boeing 737s, of which the first was delivered on 14 July 1972. For use on its long-haul routes (such as that to Paris) the airline ordered a Boeing 747-2H7B, which was delivered on 26 February 1981. Currently 12 points are served in Africa, plus a domestic network and international flights to Geneva, London, Marseilles, Paris and Rome.

Fleet:
Boeing 707
Boeing 737
Boeing 747
Hawker Siddeley HS.748

Cargolux

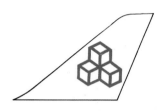

On 4 March 1970 Luxair, Loftleidir and the Swedish shipping company Salenia AB plus a group of private shareholders in Luxembourg formed Cargolux Airline International SA to undertake worldwide cargo charters from its base at Findel Airport in Luxembourg. On 14 April 1970 the new airline took delivery of its first aircraft a Canadair CL-44. Operations began in May on regular services to the Middle East and Far East, Africa, the USA and Australia; charter services were also undertaken. On 6 October 1983 Cargolux leased its first Douglas DC-8-63 from Loftleidir and standardized on the type until 10 October 1980, when its first Boeing 747-2R7F(SCD) was delivered. At present the airline operates DC-8s and Model 747s on approximately the same network that it established when it was formed in 1970.

Fleet:
Boeing 747
Douglas DC-8-63

Cathay Pacific

Formed on 24 September 1946, Cathay Pacific used Douglas DC-3s to carry freight between Shanghai and Sydney. Since 1948 the Swire group has held a controlling interest in Cathay (currently 71 per cent). The airline is also associated with the Hong Kong Aircraft Engineering Co. (HAECO). On 1 April 1959 the airline took delivery of its first Lockheed L-188 Electra, and through its takeover of the BOAC associate company Hong Kong Airways on 1 July that year Cathay acquired its second turboprop type, namely the Vickers Viscount. On 8 April 1962 the airline's first jet, a Convair CV-880, entered service on the route from Hong Kong to Tokyo via Manila. Cathay Pacific's expansion programme during the late 1960s necessitated the replacement of its CV-880s and Boeing 707s, the choice falling on the Lockheed L-1011 TriStar which is currently the mainstay of the airline's fleet. The first L-1011 was delivered on 8 August 1975 and entered service on 16 September. In October 1978 the airline turned its thoughts to expanding its network to include the UK. To this end the Boeing 747-267B was ordered, and the first was delivered on 20 July 1979, services to London starting on 17 July 1980. At present Cathay operates its Boeing 747s and L-1011s on passenger and cargo services throughout the Far East, Australia, the Middle East and Europe.

Fleet:
Boeing 747
Lockheed L-1011 TriStar

Ceskoslovenskie Statni Aerolinie (CSA)

The Czech state airline CSA was formed on 28 July 1923 and began experimental services on 28 October between Prague and Uzhorod. Between 15 March 1939 and 1 March 1946 CSA was absorbed into the German airline Deutsche Lufthansa. The airline restarted in 1946 with Douglas DC-3s and Junkers Ju 52s, and by 1947 most European capitals were being served. The network was cut back in 1948 after the Communist takeover. In 1957 CSA became the first foreign airline to operate the twin-jet Tupolev Tu-104. And early in 1960 the four-turboprop Ilyushin Il-18 started to replace ageing Ilyushin Il-12s. By 1960 CSA was on the verge of becoming the first Communist airline to operate worldwide, and on 4 May 1970 CSA started its first Prague to New York service with Ilyushin Il-62s. An extensive network of routes now links Prague with Europe, the Middle and Far East, West Africa and North and South America, and the airline also operates a domestic network serving seven cities.

Fleet:
Ilyushin Il-18
Ilyushin Il-62

Tupolev Tu-134
Yakovlev Yak-40

Tupolev Tu-134s are flown on the European routes and some internal services. Il-62s augment the European services if so desired.

China Airlines

On 16 December 1959 China Airlines was formed to operate domestic charter services with two Consolidated PBY-5A Catalinas. Scheduled domestic services in Taiwan started in October 1963 with Douglas DC-3s and Curtiss C-46s, followed by international services on 2 December 1966. The airline's first jet was a Boeing 727-109 which entered service in March 1967. Three years later services to San Francisco were started with Boeing 707s. To replace and expand its long-haul network China Airlines bought the Boeing 747, the first such aircraft being delivered on 16 May 1975. On the domestic scene the Airbus A300 has been operated since 22 June 1982. The airline currently operates scheduled passenger and cargo flights to many domestic cities and to Asia, Europe and North America.

China Airlines (continued)

Fleet:
Airbus A300
Boeing 707

Boeing 737
Boeing 747
Boeing 767

Conair

Consolidated Aircraft Corporation Limited (Conair) was formed in October 1964 to take over the activities of the Danish charter operator Enterprise A/S, which had ceased trading. Operations began on 1 April 1965 with Douglas DC-7s which were used exclusively by the owner of Conair, the Spies travel organization. The airline began to replace the piston-engined DC-7s with turbojet-powered Boeing 720s on 9 June 1971, and currently the Boeings operate charter and inclusive tour flights to desti-

nations in Europe and Africa.

Fleet:
Boeing 720

Condor Flugdienst

Formed on 25 October 1961, Condor Flugdienst is a wholly-owned charter subsidiary of Lufthansa. The formation of the charter division came from the merger of Deutsche Flugdienst GmbH and Condor Luftreederei GmbH, and the airline's initial equipment was Convair CV-440s transferred from the parent company. The airline's first jets were Boeing 727-30s also transferred from Lufthansa (in April 1965) to supplement the Vickers Viscounts then being operated. Condor had the distinction of being the first charter airline to fly the Boeing 747-30 when its first example of this aircraft was delivered on 2 April 1971.

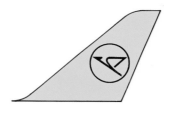

Currently Condor operates the Douglas DC-10-30 on long-haul charter work (to North America and the Far East) and the Boeing 727 and 737 plus the Airbus A300 (in the summer months) mainly to the Mediterranean, East Africa, the Canaries and the Black Sea area.

Fleet:
Airbus A300/A310

Boeing 727
Boeing 737
Douglas DC-10-30

Condor Flugdienst is the charter subsidiary of Lufthansa and operates aircraft transferred from that airline. Its major type is the Douglas DC-10.

Continental Air Lines

What is now Continental Air Lines started mail flight operations as Varney Air Lines on 6 April 1926, but was taken over by United Air Lines on 30 June 1930. The entity separated in 1934 to become Varney Air Transport. On 1 September 1937 the name was changed once again to Continental Air Lines. During World War II the airline carried out military work within the USA. After the war the airline bought Convair CV-240s in 1948 to expand its domestic network. On 10 May 1958 Continental took delivery of its first two Vickers Viscounts, and these new turboprop airliners took over many of the routes then flown by the Douglas DC-6; the Boeing 707s which started to arrive on 19 April 1959 replaced the Douglas DC-7s. On 9 September 1969 transpacific flights from Chicago to Hawaii started, thus becoming an overseas carrier. Continental's first wide-bodied aircraft was the Boeing 747, of which the first was delivered on 18 May 1970, but this type has since been replaced by the Douglas DC-10. The airline is now owned by Texas Air, which merged Texas International with Continental in October 1982. The airline's network currently serves destinations coast-to-coast in the USA, and internationally to Australia, New Zealand, Mexico and Venezuela.

Fleet:
Boeing 727
Douglas DC-9
Douglas DC-10

Continental now uses the Douglas DC-10 on many routes throughout America. It also serves destinations in South America and the Pacific.

CP Air

When Canadian Pacific Railways bought and merged 11 bush airlines on 30 January 1942, it formed Canadian Pacific Airlines. After World War II 17 converted Douglas C-47s were acquired, but very little progress with expansion was made until the airline was awarded routes to the Far East and Australia in the summer of 1949, when Canadair C-4s began services to Hong Kong and Sydney. On 16 October 1953 South American services to Mexico City and Lima were started with Douglas DC-6Bs from Vancouver. On 9 April 1958 CP Air's first

CP Air (continued)

Bristol Britannia was delivered, and the type was used on the airline's transpolar service to Amsterdam. After unsuccessful attempts in 1950 to operate the the de Havilland Comet the airline started jet services with Douglas DC-8-43s in February 1961. In the latter part of 1968 the current name was adopted, together with the present colour scheme. CP Air now operates two widebodied types, namely the Boeing 747 (first delivered in November 1973) and Douglas DC-10. The airline's domestic network is operated between numerous Canadian cities, and international services are flown to the USA, South America, Australia and Europe. Charter flights are operated to the southern USA, the West Indies and Mexico.

Fleet:
Boeing 737
Boeing 747
Douglas DC-10-30

Crossair

Scheduled services by Crossair commenced on 2 July 1979, though this Swiss third-level airline had been formed on 14 February 1975 as Business Flyers Basel; the current title was adopted on 14 November 1978. The airline operates Saab-Fairchild 340As and Swearingen SA227AC Metro IIIs on scheduled services from Zürich to Berne, Lugano, Klagenfurt, Innsbruck, Luxembourg, Strasbourg and Basle; from Berne to Paris; from Geneva to Strasbourg, Basle and Lugano; from Lugano to Berne and Venice; and from Basle to Brussels, Munich, Amsterdam and Frankfurt.

Fleet:
Saab-Fairchild 340
Swearingen Metro III

Cruzeiro do Sul

Formed as Condor Syndicat on 3 February 1927, this airline changed its named when it became a subsidiary of Deutsche Luft Hansa on 1 December 1927. During the 1930s services to Chile and Argentina were launched with Junkers Ju 52/3m aircraft. In August 1941 the airline changed its name to

Cruzeiro flies a large network around Brazil and the neighbouring countries. Highest density aircraft is the Airbus A300.

Cruzeiro do Sul (continued)

Servicos Aéreos Condor, and in December 1941 temporarily ceased trading until April 1942, when it became known as Servicos Aéreos Cruzeiro do Sul. During the 1950s Cruzeiro operated a large fleet of Douglas DC-3s and Convairliners, which were supplemented by the airline's first jet, a Sud-Aviation Caravelle, in December 1962. In July 1967 the airline took delivery of its first turboprop aircraft, a NAMC YS-11. With these two new acquisitions in service the older aircraft were slowly retired. In January 1971 the first Boeing 727s were delivered, followed by Boeing 737s in

January 1975. Since May 1975 Cruzeiro do Sul has been owned by VARIG but it still operates independently. In June 1980 the airline took delivery of the Airbus A300, and with the two Boeing types currently operates scheduled passenger and cargo services to 23 destinations in Brazil, and to seven points in the neighbouring countries.

Fleet:
Airbus A300
Boeing 727
Boeing 737

Cubana

Empresa Consolidada Cubana de Aviación started operations on 27 June 1961, although its history can be traced back to 8 October 1929 when the Curtiss group formed the Compania Nacional Cubana Aviación Curtiss CA. The airline's first international routes began with a Douglas DC-3 service between Havana and Miami, transatlantic services to Lisbon starting on 26 April 1948 with Douglas DC-4s. The first turboprop aircraft to be delivered, on 16 May 1956, was a Vickers Viscount. On 16 February 1959 Fidel Castro took control of Cuba and the airline's fleet since that time has gradually been replaced by Soviet airliners. Piston-engined Ilyushin Il-14s arrived

in 1960, followed by Il-18s in 1963. The first pure jet to be flown was the Il-62, which commenced services in November 1974 between Havana and Madrid. Currently, international passenger and cargo services are operated from Havana to Barbados, Berlin, Georgetown, Grenada, Kingston, Lima, Luanda, Madrid, Panama City, Port of Spain, Prague and Tripoli; there is a domestic network serving seven destinations.

Fleet:
Antonov An-24
Antonov An-26
Ilyushin Il-18

Ilyushin Il-62
Ilyushin Il-76
Tupolev Tu-154
Yakovlev Yak-40

Cyprus Airways

On 24 September 1947 the Cyprus government, BEA and local Cypriot interests formed Cyprus Airways. Services began with BEA Douglas DC-3s in October, and the airline's own DC-3s arrived in early 1948. The world's first scheduled turboprop service, with a Vickers Viscount 701, was operated by Cyprus Airways, in conjunction with BEA, on 18 April 1953 from London to Cyprus via Rome and Athens. From January 1958 to November 1969 BEA operated the airline's services, initially with Viscounts and later with de Havilland Comets. But from November 1969 Cyprus

Airways has operated on its own, at the start with Hawker Siddeley Tridents. Between July 1974 and September 1975 the airline did not operate, as a consequence of the Turkish invasion of the island, and after the conflict the airline moved its operations from Nicosia to Larnaca. Currently Cyprus

Cyprus Airways (continued)

Airways operates passenger and cargo flights with its fleet of Airbus A310, BAC One-Eleven and Boeing 707 aircraft to 10 destinations in Europe and to 10 points in the Middle East.

Fleet:
Airbus A310
BAC One-Eleven
Boeing 707

Dan-Air

Dan-Air was founded by Davis and Newman Ltd on 21 May 1953, originally to operate charter flights. But in June 1955, and using a Douglas DC-3, the airline began scheduled services between Blackbushe and Jersey. Since that time Dan-Air has built up a considerable charter and inclusive tour business from 13 regional UK cities and from West Berlin. In April 1972 Skyways International was acquired by Dan-Air, bringing with it many scheduled routes. On 9 May 1966 the air line's first jet aircraft, a de Havilland Comet 4, was bought and the airline's inclusive tour work was accordingly increased. Currently the airline operates scheduled passenger and cargo services domestically to 17 points, plus international services to numerous destinations in Europe. Additionally a very extensive charter and inclusive tour network is operated.

Fleet:
BAe 146
BAC One-Eleven
Boeing 727
Boeing 737
Hawker Siddeley HS.748

Dan-Air is a major operator of the British Aerospace 146, and flies these extremely quiet aircraft around the UK and Europe.

Delta Air Lines

In 1925 the world's first crop-dusting company was formed as Huff Daland Dusters. This company then began passenger operations, on 16 June 1929, between Atlanta (Georgia) and Birmingham (Alabama), under the name Delta Air Service. In 1934 the name Delta Air Corporation was adopted, though this was changed in 1945

Lockheed TriStars form the bulk of Delta's high-density fleet, but are being supplemented by Boeing 767s.

Delta Air Lines (continued)

to Delta Air Lines. The airline's first Douglas DC-3 was delivered in November 1940, and during the early part of World War II Delta flew DC-3s and Lockheed L-10As. On 1 May 1953 Chicago and Southern Air Lines merged with Delta, bringing many new routes, including international services, plus many Convair CV-340s and Lockheed L-649As. On 18 September the first Douglas DC-8-11 entered service, between New York and Atlanta, and Delta was the first operator in the world to fly the Douglas DC-9, on 8 December 1966. By 1969 Delta was an all-jet operator with 129 aircraft. The first wide-body airliner, a Boeing 747-132, was delivered on 26 September 1970. On 1

August 1972 Northeast Airlines merged with Delta, this amalgamation bringing with it many new routes in the east of the USA, and services to Bahamas and Bermuda. A new service to London (Gatwick) from Atlanta was started on 1 May 1978 with two leased Lockheed L-1011 TriStar 200s. It should be recorded that Delta has operated all the major types of Douglas commercial aircraft and, excluding the Airbus A300 series, all the wide-bodied airliners built in the West. Currently the airline operates an extensive domestic network and international services to Montreal, the Bahamas, Bermuda, San Juan, London and Frankfurt.

Fleet:
Boeing 727
Boeing 737
Boeing 757

Boeing 767
Douglas DC-8
Douglas DC-9
Lockheed L-1011 TriStar

DLT

Formed on 1 October 1974 by the reorganization of the airline OLT (Ostfriesische Lufttransport), DLT operates third-level services within West Germany and on behalf of Lufthansa (which holds a 26-per cent shareholding). DLT operates scheduled domestic services plus international flights to Amersterdam, Basle, Geneva, Venice and Zurich. The airline has a fleet of six Hawker Siddeley 748s, the first (a leased aircraft) entering service with the airline in December 1980.

Fleet:
Hawker Siddeley HS.748
Swearingen SA226

Eastern Air Lines

Pitcairn Aviation Inc. was formed in 1927, and began mail-carrying flights on 1 May 1928. Following a takeover in 1930, the airline was renamed Eastern Air Transport on 17 January 1930, and on 29 March 1938 the current title was adopted. In 1934 the airline introduced the Douglas DC-2 on the New York to Miami route, the DC-3 following on 16 January 1937. After World War II the first Lockheed Constellation was delivered on 13 May 1947. Twelve years later, on 12 January 1959, Eastern Air Lines was the first airline in the world to operate the turboprop-powered Lockheed L-188 Electra, in this instance between New York and Miami. On 24 January 1960 the first

pure jet, a Douglas DC-8-20, en´ ed service, and on 1 February 1965 Eastern was the first to operate the Boeing 727 this aircraft entering service initially on the Miami, Washington and Philadelphia routes. The first wide-body airliner operated, on 20 November 1970, was a Boeing 747 leased from Pan Am. This type was not adopted by

Eastern Air Lines (continued)

One of the world's largest airlines, Eastern flies to over 100 destinations in the Americas. It is the only US operator of the Airbus A300.

the airline, which instead ordered the Lockheed L-1011 TriStar which entered service on 26 April 1972 between Miami and New York. On 1 January 1983 Eastern was the first airline to commence services with the Boeing 757. Eastern Air Lines currently employs 37,500 staff, its head office being located at Miami, and it serves over 100 destinations in 34 states of the USA, and flies international services to the Bahamas, Bermuda, Canada, Mexico and points in the Caribbean, and in South America to Asuncion, Barranquilla, Bogota, Buenos Aires, Cali, Guayaquil, Lima, La Paz, Panama City, Quito and Santiago.

Fleet:
Airbus A300
Boeing 727
Boeing 757
Douglas DC-9
Lockheed L-1011 TriStar

East West Airlines

Operations by East West Airlines began between Sydney and Tamworth on 23 June 1947, using Avro Ansons. The airline acquired Douglas DC-3s in 1953, and these have since been replaced by Fokker F.27s. On 26 August 1959 East West commenced services between Sydney and Tamworth with the Friendship, which until recently has been the mainstay of its fleet. On 15 April 1983 the airline's first jet was delivered, a Fokker F.28 Mk 4000, and this type is now replacing some of the F.27s. Recently Skywest Airlines acquired East West, and the combined airline now covers

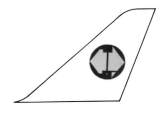

a route network to every state in Australia.

Fleet:
Beech Queen Air
Fokker F.27
Fokker F.28

Ecuatoriana

The national airline of Ecuador was formed in July 1974 to take over from the Compania Ecuatoriana de Aviación SA, which had been formed in May 1957. Ecuatoriana currently flies from Quito and Guayaquil to Miami, New York, Los Angeles, Caracas, Santiago, Panama City, Cali, Lima, Mexico City, Bogota, Rio de Janeiro, Sao Paulo and

Ecuatoriana (continued)

Buenos Aires. Supplementing the Boeing 707s and 720s are two leased Douglas DC-10-30s, the first delivered in September 1983. Engineering, technical and commercial assistance is given by Israel Aircraft Industries.

Fleet:
Boeing 707

Boeing 720
Douglas DC-10-30

Egypt Air

The history of Egypt Air can be traced to Misr Airwork, which was formed on 7 June 1932. Operations began in July 1933 with de Havilland D.H.84 Dragons between Cairo and Mersa Matruh. International service started in 1934 to Haifa. In 1949 Airwork relinquished its interest and the airline became known as Misrair SAE. In March 1951 three Vickers Viscounts were ordered, and the first of these entered service on 16 March 1956. Just over four years later, on 10 June 1960, the first pure jet airliner, a de Havilland Comet 4C, was delivered. On 23 December 1960 Misrair amalgamated with Syrian Airways to form United Arab Airlines, but the Syrians left UAA in 1961 and UAA formed the domestic carrier Misrair in 1964. During the 1960s and early 1970s numerous Soviet types were used by the airline, namely the Antonov An-24, Ilyushin Il-18 and Il-62, and Tupolev Tu-154, but all these have now been replaced. On 10 October 1971 the airline adopted its current title and colour scheme. To replace the Soviet aircraft Boeing 737s and Airbus

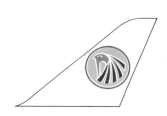

A300s were initially leased and later purchased. The Western equipment started to arrive in October 1975 and April 1977 respectively. Egypt Air currently operates a domestic network (under the name of Misrair) and an international schedule that includes destinations in Africa, East and West Europe, and Asia as far as Bombay, Bangkok, Hong Kong and Tokyo.

Fleet:
Airbus A300
Boeing 707
Boeing 737
Boeing 747
Boeing 767
Fokker F.27

El Al

Formed on 11 November 1948 with aircraft transferred from the Israel Air Transport Command, El Al flew its first service on 31 July 1949, between Tel Aviv and Paris. Services to New York began on 16 May 1951 with a Lockheed L-049. El Al's only turboprop airliner was the Bristol Britannia, which started services between Tel Aviv and New York on 22 December 1959. Further modernization took place in December 1960, when a leased VARIG Boeing 707 entered service. From the mid 1960s until 1971 the airline operated only Boeing 707s and 720s. But on 26 May 1971 the first Boeing 747 was delivered. To-

gether with the Boeing 767 (first delivered on 12 July 1983) and Boeing 707, the Boeing 747 operates El Al's long-haul and high-density flights to Europe, North America, and Africa. For its short-haul routes the airline operates two Boeing 737s.

Airbus A300s were bought by Egypt Air to replace Ilyushin Il-62s supplied by the Soviet Union following the change of political allegiance.

El Al (continued)

Fleet:
Boeing 707
Boeing 737
Boeing 747
Boeing 767

El Al has recently begun cargo operations with this Boeing 747. Other 747s operate the long-haul routes but Boeing 767s are being phased in on European services.

Ethiopian Airlines

Formed by the proclamation of Emperor Haile Selassie on 26 December 1945, with technical assistance from Trans World Airlines, Ethiopian Airlines began operation with five Douglas C-47s on 8 April 1946. On 8 November 1960 Ethiopian Airlines flew a Douglas DC-6B on its first service from Addis Ababa to Accra, so becoming the first African airline to fly from east to west across the continent. In November 1962 two Boeing 720s were delivered. To replace DC-6s the airline bought Boeing 727s, the first being delivered on 18 September 1979. On its domestic and regional routes the airline still uses Douglas DC-3s, but these are being gradually replaced by de Havilland Canada DHC-6s and DHC-7s. To replace the Boeing 720 and 707 on longer-distance international flights, Ethiopian Air-

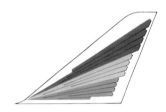

lines has bought the Boeing 767; the first was delivered on 23 May 1984. At present a domestic network serves 40 towns, and internationally Ethiopian Airlines serves destinations in Europe, the Middle and Far East, and North Africa.

Fleet:
Boeing 707
Boeing 720

Ethiopian Airlines serves many destinations in the Middle East, North Africa and Europe as well as a large domestic network. Flagship aircraft is the Boeing 767.

Ethiopian Airlines (continued)

Boeing 727
Boeing 767
de Havilland Canada DHC-5

de Havilland Canada DHC-6
de Havilland Canada DHC-7
Douglas DC-3

Europe Aero Service

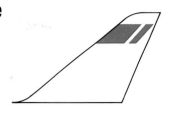

Formed in July 1965 as a subsidiary of the Société Aero Sahara, Europe Aero Service began scheduled passenger operations one year later with Handley Page Heralds between Perpignan and Palma (Majorca). On 19 April 1972 the airline took delivery of its first Vickers Vanguard, and this type was used for charter work and scheduled services within France and to European destinations. In February 1978 the airline's first jet, a Sud-Aviation Caravelle, was delivered and this type has become the mainstay of the fleet. The airline's main tasks are charter flights and operating services for Air Inter and Air Charter International, but some scheduled flights within France and to Spain are also undertaken.

Fleet:
Boeing 727
Sud-Aviation Caravelle

Faucett

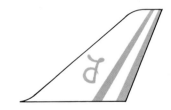

Formed on 15 September 1928 by a US citizen named Elmer J. Faucett, Compania de Aviacion Faucett operated its initial domestic services with two Stinson Detroiters. During the 1950s and 1960s Faucett operated Douglas DC-3s, DC-4s and DC-6s. The airline's first jet was a Boeing 727-63 acquired from Braniff on 9 April 1968. Although Faucett is one of the oldest South American airlines, it still operates only domestic passenger flights with a varied fleet of jet aircraft and two Britten-Norman Islanders. Cargo flights to Panama City and Miami are undertaken with leased Boeing 707s. Passenger and cargo charters are also undertaken. The airline's majority shareholder, since 1982, is Aeronaves del Peru, which has a 59 per cent interest.

Fleet:
Boeing 707
Boeing 727
Britten-Norman Islander
Douglas DC-8

Federal Express Corporation

In 1972 Frederick W. Smith formed a small package freight air carrier named Federal Express. Services commenced on 17 April 1973 with specially converted Dassault Falcon 20Ds from the company's base at Memphis. By the end of the first year of operations there were 25 Falcon 20Ds serving 50 destinations. As a result of the deregulation of cargo flights in the USA in November 1977 Federal Express was able to expand, and to this end the airline bought Boeing 727-22s from United Airlines; the

Federal Express Corporation (continued)

first was delivered on 11 January 1978. With this operator's introduction of the Boeing 727 business expanded enormously, and to cope with the extra work Douglas DC-10-30CFs were purchased, the first arriving in March 1980. At present the company operates from its hub at Memphis on nightly services to 280 points in the USA and Canada, and is shortly to expand its operations to Europe with a base at Stansted Airport, north of London.

Fleet:
Boeing 727
Cessna Caravan
Dassault Falcon 20
Douglas DC-10

Finnair

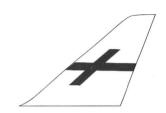

One of the world's oldest airlines, Finnair was formed as Aero O/Y by Consul Bruno Lucander on 1 November 1923. At first only domestic services were operated, but 2 June 1924 saw the start of the first international service, from Helsinki to Stockholm. It was not until 15 June 1937 that the airline operated its first landplane, a de Havilland D.H.89 Dragon Rapide, from Riga to Liepaja. In 1946 the Finnish government took a 70 per cent holding in the airline (currently the state holding is 76 per cent). After the war Finnair purchased Douglas DC-3s and Convair CV-240s, and with these aircraft it began to expand its network within Europe. To replace the ageing Convairs, Finnair bought the Sud-Aviation Caravelle IA, the first being delivered on 18 February 1960. The Caravelle remained in service until 30 April 1983. Finnair did not expand outside Europe until January 1969, when the first Douglas DC-8-62 was delivered, shortly afterwards entering service between Helsinki and New York. The main-stay of the short-haul fleet is at present the Douglas DC-9, which operates in Europe. For long-haul flights to cities such as Los Angles, Tokyo and Montreal the airline uses the Douglas DC-10-30. An extensive domestic network is operated to more than 20 destinations using the DC-9s and Fokker F.27s, shortly to be joined by ATR 42s.

Fleet:
Aérospatiale/Aeritalia ATR42
Douglas DC-8
Douglas DC-9
Douglas DC-10
Fokker F.27

The Douglas DC-10 is Finnair's largest type, and it flies these on the long-haul scheduled flights around the world.

Flying Tigers

The National Skyways Freight Corporation was formed on 25 June 1945 to operate all-cargo flights. Upon formation the airline operated Budd RB-1s, but these were soon replaced by Douglas DC-3s and DC-4s, and Curtiss C-46s. The company took its current name in 1946. In the 1950s Flying Tigers used Douglas DC-6s and Lockheed L-1049Hs. During the early days of the airline charter services were operated on behalf of the military across the Pacific, and gradually Flying Tigers built up a scheduled network within the USA. On 31 May 1961 the airline started using the turboprop-powered Canadair CL-44, which was ideal for cargo operators in that it had a fully swinging tail unit. The company's first jet, a Boeing 707, was delivered on 19 March 1966, but this type was replaced by the Douglas DC-8-63 from 1968. Scheduled cargo services across the Pacific started in 1969. Eleven years after receiving the 707 the airline's first Boeing 747 was delivered, on 2 April 1977, and was then converted to all-

cargo configuration. On 1 October 1980 Flying Tigers absorbed Seaboard World Airlines, thereby gaining access to the North Atlantic and European markets. Flying Tigers owns a passenger subsidiary called Tower Air, which was formed in March 1983. Flying Tigers currently operates worldwide scheduled and charter cargo flights with its fleet of Boeing 747s and Douglas DC-8s. On domestic services it uses Boeing 727s.

Fleet:
Boeing 727
Boeing 747
Douglas DC-8

Flying Tigers operates a worldwide cargo service with the Boeing 747 as the major type. This Boeing 727 is typical of those used on domestic services.

Frontier Airlines

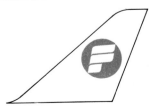

The origins of the Denver-based Frontier Airlines can be traced to 1946, when Monarch Airlines was formed with Douglas DC-3 aircraft. On 1 June 1950 Monarch and two smaller airlines merged to form Frontier Airlines. To replace the DC-3s, Convair CV-340s were purchased in 1959, and these were later converted to turbo-prop power, thereby becoming Convair CV-580s. In September 1966 the airline's first jet entered service, a Boeing 727, and this

type began to replace the Convairs. Further expansion was made in October 1967 when Central Airlines was taken over, this making Frontier one of the largest US

Frontier Airlines (continued)

regional carriers. The mainstay of the airline's current fleet is a total of 51 Boeing 737s (the first of these was accepted on 20 May 1969) and there are five Douglas DC-9-80s. The airline operates to 26 states, covering points ranging from Detroit and Atlanta in the east to the Pacific coast of the USA, and flies services to Canada and Mexico.

Fleet:
Boeing 737
Douglas DC-9

Garuda Indonesian Airways

On 21 December 1949 the governments of Indonesia and the Netherlands jointly formed the present-day Garuda Indonesian Airways, although the airline's history can be traced back to October 1938 when KLM formed KNILM. The newly-formed airline started with Douglas DC-3s and Consolidated Catalinas, which were supplemented in September 1950 by the airline's first Convair CV-240. On 12 July 1954 the airline was nationalized. To help modernize the fleet Lockheed Electras were ordered and the first was delivered on 14 January 1961, followed in September 1963 by Garuda's first jet equipment, namely the Convair CV-990. Services to Amsterdam were started in March 1965. The domestic and regional fleet was updated in 1969 by the arrival of the Douglas DC-9-30 and Fokker F.27, the latter being replaced later by F.28s. To replace some of its Douglas DC-8s, the airline purchased Douglas DC-10-30s, though leased examples were at first operated from October 1973. To help expand passenger capacity on its international and regional routes, the airline bought Boeing 747s and Airbus A300s. Currently passenger and cargo flights are flown to Europe, the Far East and Australia, while a domestic network serves 30 destinations. Garuda owns Merpati Nusantara, which was bought on 1 January 1963 and still operates under its own name.

Fleet:
Airbus A300
Boeing 747

Douglas DC-9
Fokker F.28

High-density routes have been expanded by Garuda with the introduction of the Airbus A300. These serve mainly on internal and local international flights.

Ghana Airways

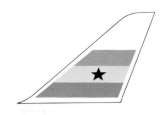

Formed on 4 July 1958 by the Ghanaian government and BOAC, Ghana Airways began international services on 16 July with leased BOAC aircraft. The first aircraft that Ghana Airways owned was a Bristol Britannia which entered service in 1960. On 14 February 1961 the airline became totally state owned. Between 1961 and 1964 Ghana Airways operated Ilyushin Il-18s. To replace the Britannia and Il-18s two Vickers VC10s were bought in 1965, and these have now been superseded by a single Douglas DC-10-30 delivered on 24 February 1983, this replaced KLM examples which had been leased since 1980. Currently the airline flies to London and Rome in Europe with its DC-10, while regional and domestic services are flown by the Douglas DC-9 and Fokker F-28s.

Fleet:
Douglas DC-9
Douglas DC-10
Fokker F.28

Gulf Air

On 24 March 1950 Gulf Aviation was formed to operate Avro Ansons in the Persian Gulf area. In October 1951 it became a subsidiary of BOAC, which helped the airline to buy larger and more modern equipment. For the regional and oil state destinations Fokker F.27s were acquired in February 1967, followed in November 1969 by BAC One-Elevens. In April 1970, using leased BOAC Vickers VC10s, services from the Gulf to London were started. On 1 April 1974 the Gulf states of Bahrain, Oman, Qatar and the United Arab Emirates formed Gulf Air, which initially operated the aircraft owned by Gulf Aviation. Currently the airline operates two types, namely the Boeing 737 (introduced in June 1977) and the Lockheed L-1011 TriStar (first delivered in January 1976). An affiliated airline, Oman Aviation Services, was formed on 24 May 1981 and operates a short-haul network, whereas Gulf Air now flies to Europe, and the Middle and Far East.

Fleet:
Boeing 737
Lockheed L-1011 TriStar

As well as a short-haul network, Gulf Air also flies Lockheed TriStars to destinations in Europe. The colour scheme is striking.

Hapag-Lloyd

The German charter and inclusive tour operator Hapag-Lloyd began activities with three Boeing 727-81s in March 1973 after being formed in March 1972 as a subsidiary of the German shipping company of the same name. In January 1979 Bavaria/Germanair was taken over and in the same year, on 3 April, the airline's first Airbus A300 was delivered. Currently the airline operates A300s, Boeing 727s and Boeing 737s on charter flights to southern and eastern Europe plus West Africa and the Canary Islands.

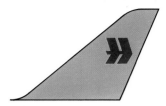

Fleet:
Airbus A300
Boeing 727
Boeing 737

Iberia

Formed on 7 July 1940, Iberia took over from CLASSA, LAPE and TAE. It was owned by the Spanish government and Deutsche Luft Hansa until 1943, when it became totally state-owned. Douglas DC-3s were first operated in 1944, followed by Douglas DC-4s in 1946 for use on the long-haul routes e.g. Madrid to Buenos Aires. The airline's first jet was a Douglas DC-8 which entered service between Madrid and New York on 2 July 1961. On European services Iberia started to use the Sud-Aviation Caravelle on 1 May 1962, replacing the Convair CV-440s that were then being operated. Iberia's first wide-body airliner was the Boeing 747, which entered service late in 1970. Currently the airline operates

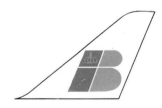

scheduled passenger and cargo flights to all the main cities in Europe using mainly Boeing 727s, Douglas DC-9s, and Airbus A300s. On the airline's long-haul services to the Americas, the Middle East and Africa Boeing 747s and Douglas DC-10s are the main aircraft operated. Closely connected with Iberia is Aviaco, which is owned by the same government agency.

Fleet:
Airbus A300
Boeing 727

Boeing 747
Douglas DC-9
Douglas DC-10

Boeing 747s operate the long haul routes to North and South America whilst Airbus A300s, Boeing 727s and Douglas DC-10s fly the shorter sectors.

Icelandair

Icelandair traces its history to 3 June 1937, when Flufelag Akureyrar was founded with a single Waco floatplane. International services began on 27 May 1946 between Iceland and Copenhagen via Prestwick, and services to London started on 3 May 1949. In 1956 the airline was renamed Icelandair. The airline's Douglas DC-4s were replaced on scheduled work by the Vickers Viscount in May 1957, and 10 years later in June 1967 the first Boeing 727 was delivered. On 1 August 1973 Icelandair and Loftledir merged but remained operationally separate until 1 October 1979. Scheduled passenger and cargo services are currently flown to the United States of America, Western Europe, the Faroes and Greenland, and there is a domestic network flown by Fokker F.27s. Charter work is also undertaken.

Fleet:
Boeing 727
Douglas DC-8
Fokker F.27

Indian Airlines

Formed when all Indian airlines were nationalized on 28 May 1953, Indian Airlines began services on 1 August of that year with many types that had been taken over from other airlines. On 10 October 1957 the first Vickers Viscount entered service, and supplementing the Viscount in February 1964 was the airline's first pure jet, the Sud-Aviation Caravelle. Indian Airlines is the Indian domestic and regional carrier and currently operates Fokker F.27 Friendships and Indian-built HS 748s on shorter routes and to more remote destinations. On the longer high-density routes Boeing 737s (first delivered on 9 November 1970) and Airbus A300s (first entered service in December 1976) are operated.

Fleet:
Airbus A300
Boeing 737
Fokker F.27
Hawker Siddeley HS.748

Inex Adria

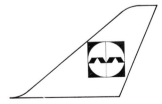

Adria Aviopromet was formed in March 1961 by the Yugoslav government to carry out charter and inclusive tour services. Operations began in March 1962 with four ex-KLM Douglas DC-6Bs. The airline's current title, Inex Adria, was adopted in 1968 when the original airline was reorganized, and the airline's present mainstay is the Douglas DC-9. The first of these, a Series 32, was delivered on 25 April 1969. Although the airline's main tasks are charter and inclusive tours, it also operates domestic flights which link its base at Ljubljana with Belgrade, Sarajevo, Skopje, Split and Titograd, plus an international service to Larnaca. Inex Adria also operates two de Havilland Canada DHC-7s on domestic services.

Fleet:
de Havilland Canada DHC-7
Douglas DC-9

Interflug

Established as Deutsche Lufthansa on 1 July 1955, the new airline operated its first scheduled service on 4 February 1956 with an Ilyushin Il-14. Domestic services from East Berlin did not start until 16 June 1957. Due to confusion with the West German operator of the same name, the East German airline adopted the title Interflug for its flights to Western Europe on 18 September 1958; the airline did not completely lose its old name until September 1963. Early in 1961 the first three turboprop Ilyushin Il-18s were delivered, and these are still in service. The first pure jet Interflug operated on a regular basis was the Tupolev Tu-134, which entered service in 1967. The Tu-134 is currently the mainstay of the airline's fleet, but also in use is the Ilyushin

Il-62 for high-density and long-haul routes. The first of this latter type entered service in 1970. A separate division of Interflug, Agraflug, undertakes agricultural and survey work, and has a large fleet of helicopters. Currently Interflug operates scheduled passenger and cargo flights to 50 cities in 36 countries in Europe, Africa, the Middle and Far East, and Central America, plus charter services.

Fleet:
Ilyushin Il-18

Ilyushin Il-62
Tupolev Tu-134

Iran Air

On 2 November 1961 Iranian Airways and Persian Air Services merged to form United Iranian Airways. Iranian Airways had been formed in December 1944 with Douglas DC-3s and progressed to Vickers Viscounts in March 1958, with services mainly to the Middle East. Persian Air Services had started operations in February 1957 with Avro Yorks, and concentrated mainly on cargo and passenger charter flights; immediately before the merger in August 1961 it had started operating leased Boeing 707s on flights to Brussels, Geneva, London and Paris. The first wide-body jet used by the airline was a Boeing 747SP-86 delivered on 12 March 1976. A further wide-body type used by the airline on its services mainly to neighbouring countries is the Airbus A300;

the first of these was delivered, on lease, on 7 March 1978. Since the change of regime in Iran and the war with Iraq the airline's fleet has altered very little but its network has been contracted. Passenger and cargo flights are operated to 18 points domestically, mainly with Boeing 727s and 737s, and to 16 destinations in Asia, Europe and the Middle East, for which the A300s and Boeing 747s are mainly operated.

Operating mainly to Europe, Iran Air's Boeing 747SPs provide a fast link between Tehran and London, Paris and Brussels.

Iran Air (continued)

Fleet:

Airbus A300	Boeing 727
Boeing 707	Boeing 737
	Boeing 747

Iraqi Airways

Formed by the government-owned Iraqi State Railways in December 1945, Iraqi Airways initially operated de Havilland D.H.89A Dragon Rapides. Technical assistance for the new airline was given by BOAC, which also leased to it Douglas DC-3s and Vickers Vikings. On 13 October 1955 the first Vickers Viscount was delivered and shortly afterwards entered service on the London route. On 1 April 1960 Iraqi Airways gained its independence from the railways. To replace the Viscounts three Hawker Siddeley Tridents were ordered, and the first entered service in November 1965. For the next nine years the Viscounts and Tridents operated the airline's services until the airline ordered four types of Boeing, namely the Models 707, 727, 737 and 747 in 1974, all these types entering service

between 1974 and 1976. Iraqi Airways also took into its inventory three types of Soviet aircraft, namely the Antonov An-12 and An-24 in 1969 and 1970, and the Ilyushin Il-76 in 1978. At present the airline operates scheduled passenger and cargo flights to Asia, Europe, the Middle East, North Africa and Latin America, plus a domestic route system.

Fleet:

Boeing 707	Boeing 737
Boeing 727	Boeing 747
	Ilyushin Il-76

Ilyushin Il-76s are operated by Iraqi Airways on cargo flights. These aircraft have a military capability and still possess a rear gun turret.

Japan Air Lines

On 1 August 1951 Japanese Air Lines was formed by private interests, and started domestic operations on 10 October 1951. This new airline took over from Great Japan (Dai Nippon) Air Lines which had ceased operations in 1945. In October 1953 the company was reorganized as Japan Air Lines (or NKKK). The first jet to be delivered to the airline was a Douglas DC-8-32 on 16 July 1960, the type entering service on 12 August 1960 between Tokyo and San Francisco. As a joint operation Japan Air Lines and Aeroflot started flights between Tokyo and Moscow on 17 April 1967, initially using the Tupolev Tu-114 turboprop and later the Ilyushin Il-62. The first wide-body airliner operated by JAL was the Boeing 747, of which the first was delivered on 22 April 1970, followed by the Douglas DC-10-40 in April 1976. Japan Air Lines is the largest operator of the Boeing 747, with 54 in service or on order at the present time.

Currently 60 per cent of the airline is controlled by private interests, the balance being held by the Japanese government. Japan Air Lines operates its fleet of Boeing and Douglas airliners on a network of routes worldwide. Subsidiary airlines are Japan Asia Airways and Southwest Air Lines.

Fleet:
Boeing 727
Boeing 747
Douglas DC-8
Douglas DC-10

Japan Air Lines is one of the few operators of the Series 40 variant of the Douglas DC-10. These are used on long-range routes worldwide.

JAT

The Yugoslav state airline JAT (Jugoslovenski Aerotransport) operated its first revenue service on 1 April 1947 with a Douglas DC-3, although the airline can be traced back to November 1945 when it was part of the Yugoslav air force. To expand the airline's scheduled and charter services two Douglas DC-6Bs were delivered in November 1957: the airline thus has the distinction of receiving the last Douglas DC-6s to be produced. To replace the DC-6BS three Sud-Aviation Caravelle VINs were ordered, and the first was accepted on 11 January 1963. With this new aircraft JAT

expanded its network to include Copenhagen, Warsaw and Moscow. In April 1969 two Douglas DC-9s were leased pending the delivery of JAT's own aircraft; the new type replaced the Caravelle on international routes, the older jet being redeployed to

JAT (continued)

Widely used throughout Europe, JAT's DC-9 fleet will soon be supplemented by Boeing 737-300s.

domestic routes. On long-haul routes JAT operates Boeing 707s and Douglas DC-10-30s; the first of the latter was delivered on 8 December 1978. In the near future JAT will take delivery of its first Boeing 737-300s, which will take over some of the short-haul routes currently operated by DC-9s. At present JAT and Avio-Taxi operate scheduled passenger and cargo flights to 16 points domestically and to nearly 40 cities in Europe, the Middle East, North Africa, North America and Australia.

Fleet:
Boeing 707
Boeing 747
Douglas DC-9
Douglas DC-10

Kenya Airways

After the demise of East African Airways, Kenya Airways was formed by the Kenyan government on 22 January 1977. It began operations with two leased BMA Boeing 707-321s on 4 February 1977, with a service from London to Nairobi via Frankfurt, Rome and Athens. Domestic and regional services are carried with Douglas DC-9-32s and Fokker F.27s, both types being acquired from its predessor EAA in early 1977. At present Kenya Airways operates scheduled passenger and cargo services from Nairobi to Cairo, Athens, Rome, London, Frankfurt, Paris, Khartoum, Dubai, Jeddah, Bombay, Addis Ababa, Mogadishu, the Seychelles, Entebbe, Harare, Dar

es Salaam and Lusaka, plus domestic services to Mombasa, Malindi and Kisumu.

Fleet:
Boeing 707
Boeing 720
Fokker F.27
Douglas DC-9

KLM

The Dutch national flag carrier KLM (Koninklijke Luchtvaart Maatschappij NV), which can boast more than 60 years of continuous operation was established on 7 October 1919. The airline's first service was on 17 May 1920 from Amsterdam to London with a de Havilland D.H.16. After establishing itself in Europe during the 1920s KLM started a very adventurous service to

Djakarta on 1 October 1931. During World War II KLM's services in Europe ceased, and only the West Indian schedule con-

High density routes are flown by the Airbus A310, and these are a regular sight at London-Heathrow, Frankfurt and Paris-Charles de Gaulle.

tinued during this period. On 17 January 1945 KLM resumed its European operations, and in 1946 services to New York, Curacao and Brazil were started. In 1947 KLM began its first transpolar service from Amsterdam to Tokyo with Douglas DC-7Cs. On 6 June 1957 the first Vickers Viscount was delivered, and with the Lockheed L-188 Electra, first delivered 15 December 1959, KLM modernized its fleet. The first pure jet was a Douglas DC-8 which began flights between Amsterdam and New York on 16 April 1960. In common with many other international operators, KLM's first wide-body aircraft was a Boeing 747, of which the first was delivered on 16 January 1971. Currently the short-haul fleet consists of Douglas DC-9s which are supplemented on the high-density routes by the Airbus A310, whereas on the long-haul routes (to East Africa, the Americas, Australia and the Far East) the airline uses Boeing 747s and Douglas DC-10s. KLM holds the distinction of being the only airline in the world to have operated every type of Douglas airliner ever built, from the DC-2 to the present DC-10. KLM has four airline subsidiaries, namely KLM Aercarto, NLM City Hopper, KLM Air Charter and KLM Helicopters. It also has an interest in Martinair.

Fleet:
Airbus A310
Boeing 747
Douglas DC-8
Douglas DC-9
Douglas DC-10

Korean Air Lines

Korean National Airlines was founded in May 1947, firstly with Stinson Voyagers and later with Douglas DC-3s. After the Korean War the airline restarted in November 1951 and commenced international services from Iwakuni to Tokyo with leased Douglas DC-4s. In June 1962 the government reorganized the airline and the current title, Korean Air Lines, was adopted. In December 1963 the airline took delivery of its first turboprop airliner, the Fokker F.27, and this type is used on the airline's short-haul routes. Then on 19 July 1967 the first Douglas DC-9-32 was delivered, the type replacing the Lockheed L-1049H Constellation on the airline's Asian routes. In March 1969 the government of Korea sold the airline to private interests. The first wide-body aircraft Korean Air Lines

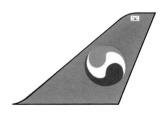

operated was the Boeing 747, the first being delivered on 1 May 1973. With the Boeing 707 and two wide-body types, the Airbus A300 and Douglas DC-10, Korean Air Lines operates long-haul and high-density routes which include destinations in Europe, the Middle and Far East, and North America; on its short-haul routes the Boeing 727, Airbus A300 and Fokker F.27 are mainly used.

Korean Air Lines (continued)

Fleet:

Airbus A300
Boeing 707
Boeing 747

Fokker F.27
Fokker F.28
Douglas DC-10

Kuwait Airways

Established by the Sheik of Kuwait and local investors in 1953, Kuwait National Airways began with Douglas DC-3s. The airline's first service, from Basra to Cairo, was flown in April 1954. On 18 September 1958 it took delivery of its first Vickers Viscount, and also in 1958 BOAC took over management of the airline; this year also saw adoption of the current title, Kuwait Airways. In 1964 the airline became state-owned, and on 2 March 1964 started operating the de Havilland Comet 4C on flights to London. The airline's first wide-body aircraft was the Boeing 747, the first being delivered on 28 July 1978; its other wide-body types are the Airbus A300 and A310, but these are to be supplemented shortly by the Boeing 767. Currently scheduled passenger and cargo

services are operated to 37 cities in 36 countries in the Middle and Far East, Europe, Africa, North America and Asia.

Fleet:

Airbus A300
Airbus A310
Boeing 707
Boeing 727
Boeing 747

LAN-Chile

Formed by the Chilean Army Air Service on 5 March 1929 as Linea Aeropostal Santiago-Arica, this pioneering airline was transferred to the government in 1932 when the current title, LAN-Chile (Linea Aérea Nacional de Chile), was adopted. It was not until 1946 that the first international services were started with Lockheed Lodestars, from Santiago to Buenos Aires; services to Miami with Douglas DC-6Bs commenced in August 1958. The airline's first jet equipment was a Sud-Aviation Caravelle VIR, of which the first was received on 6 March 1964. Just over three years later the first Boeing 707 was delivered for use on the airline's long-haul services, which by then included European destinations. Long-haul services were upgraded in December 1980 when a wide-body aircraft, a Douglas DC-10-30, was

leased from Laker Airways, and June 1982 saw the purchase of two DC-10-30s from Air New Zealand. Currently LAN-Chile operates cargo and passenger services domestically, and to seven points in South America, Miami and New York in North America, Madrid, Paris and Frankfurt in Europe, plus flights to Easter Island, Papeete and Nandi.

Fleet:

Boeing 707
Boeing 737
Douglas DC-10

Libyan Arab Airlines

In September 1964 The Kingdom of Libya Airlines was formed to take over from

Libravia and United Libyan Airlines. The new airline started operations with two

Libyan Arab Airlines (continued)

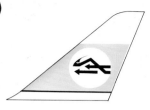

Sud-Aviation Caravelles in August 1965. Before the delivery in 1969 of its own Fokker F.27s the airline operated leased ATI F.27s on its domestic services. Shortly after the coup d'etat that ousted the king, the airline changed its name to Libyan Arab Airlines on 1 September 1969. The airline currently operates Boeing 727s and 707s on its services to 17 points in Europe, Asia and North Africa, and on its domestic and regional services the F.27 and F.28 are used. All cargo services are operated by Soviet-built Ilyushin Il-76s and some Boeing 707s.

Fleet:
Boeing 707
Boeing 727
Fokker F.27
Fokker F.28
Ilyushin Il-76

The Boeing 727 is the major type in the inventory of Libyan Arab Airlines, these being used to points in Europe, North Africa and Asia.

Linjeflyg

Scandinavian Airlines System and AB Aerotransport formed Linjeflyg on 2 April 1957 to take over from Airtaco the Swedish domestic passenger and newspaper services which it had operated since the 1950s. The airline's initial equipment was mainly Douglas DC-3s, assisted by Lockheed Lodestars and Lockheed L-12s. These types were replaced by Convair CV-440s, of which the first was delivered on 21 January 1960, and remained as the airline's main type until 1973 when the first jet-powered Fokker F.28 was delivered, on 18 May. Currently Linjeflyg operates only F.28s on its domestic services to 25 destinations in Sweden, plus charter flights to numerous points in north west Europe.

Fleet:
Fokker F.28

LOT

The Polish state-owned airline Polskie Linie Lotnicze (LOT) can trace its history to a privately-owned company formed in 1922, namely Aero Lloyd Warschau, and to Aero

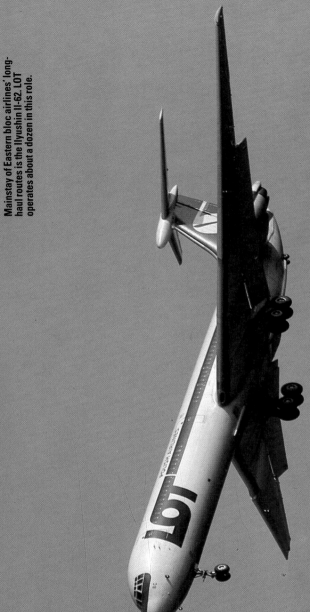

Mainstay of Eastern bloc airlines' long-haul routes is the Ilyushin Il-62. LOT operates about a dozen in this role.

LOT (continued)

TZ. On 1 January 1929 all civil airline activities were taken over by the government, and thus LOT was formed. After the German invasion on 1 September 1939 all civil flights ceased until 6 March 1945, when the airline was re-formed with 20 Lisunov Li-2s, and by the end of the first year services to London had started. During 1950s the mainstays of the fleet were the Ilyushin Il-12 and Il-14, supplemented in 1957 by five Convair CV-240s. In April 1961 and November 1962 the airline updated its fleet with the purchase of Ilyushin Il-18s and Vickers Viscounts; the former are still in service with the airline on its less prestigious flights. For use mainly on its domestic routes the airline uses a fleet of Antonov An-24s, whereas on the long-haul services to North America, the Middle East, North Africa and Asia (and on high-density routes) Ilyushin Il-62s are operated, with Tupolev Tu-134As on the short-haul services.

Fleet:
Antonov An-24
Ilyushin Il-18
Ilyushin Il-62
Tupolev Tu-134A

LTU

Founded as Lufttransport Union in 1955, the airline altered its title one year later to the current name LTU (Lufttransport-Unternetiemen KG) to avoid confusion with another operator. Charter services began in 1956 with Vickers Vikings. In August 1964 the first jet aircraft, a Sud-Aviation Caravelle 10R, was delivered. This type was replaced by the Lockheed L-1011 TriStar, the first of these wide-body airliners being delivered on 29 May 1973. The TriStar is the only type the airline currently operates. LTU concentrates its operations on inclusive tour and charter work, which takes its aircraft to points in Europe, North Africa, North America and the Caribbean.

Fleet:
Lockheed L-1011 TriStar

Lufthansa

On 6 January 1926 Deutsche Luft Hansa came into being through the merger of Deutscher Aero Lloyd and Junkers Luftverkhr. The winged crest on the fin can be traced back to 1919, when Deutsche Luftreederei was formed, this airline later being absorbed into Deutscher Aero Lloyd. By 1939 DLH was a leading European operator, with destinations in Europe, the Middle and Far East, and South America. But on 21 April 1945 the airline ceased operations with the defeat of Germany at the end of World War II. On 6 January 1953 a new airline, named Luftag, was formed. Shortly afterwards four Convair CV-340s and four Lockheed L-1049G Constellations were ordered. On 16 August 1954 the current title of Deutsche Lufthansa AG was adopted. Domestic operations began on 1 April 1955 with the Convairs, and on 8 June of the same year transatlantic services to New York were started with the Constellations. On 5 October the first turboprop-powered Vickers Viscount was delivered, and this type became the mainstay of the European fleet. On the intercontinental routes the Constellations were replaced by Boeing 707s; the first of these four-engined jets was delivered on 3 April 1960. The first wide-body airliner operated by Lufthansa

Lufthansa is a major user of the Airbus A300, using it alongside the A310 and Boeing 727 and 737 on European routes.

was the Boeing 747-130, which was handed over on 10 March 1970. Together with the Douglas DC-10-30, this forms the basis of the long-haul fleet, with destinations in Africa, the Middle and Far East, Australia and the Americas. On its shorter routes and European services, the airline uses the Airbus A300 and A310, Boeing 727 and Boeing 737. Lufthansa's airline subsidiaries are Condor Flugdienst (founded in 1961) and German Cargo (founded in 1976).

Fleet:
Airbus A300
Airbus A310
Boeing 707
Boeing 727
Boeing 737
Boeing 747
Douglas DC-10

Luxair

Luxair (Société Luxemburgeoise de navigation Aérienne) was formed in 1961 with aid from the Luxembourg government and local institutions to take over Luxembourg Airlines, which had started operations in February 1948 and ceased trading in 1958. Initially leased Fokker F.27s were used by the airline on routes to Paris, Amsterdam and Frankfurt, and these were supplemented in April 1966 by a single Vickers Viscount. The first jet, a leased Sud-Aviation Caravelle VIR, was initially operated in March 1970, and until the Boeing 737s arrived in 1977 the Caravelle was the backbone of the airline's fleet. Currently Luxair operates scheduled services to Athens, Frankfurt, London, Nice, Palma, Paris and

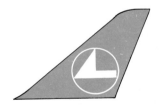

Rome with its F.27s and Boeing 737s. For its service to South Africa Boeing 707s are operated. Charter and inclusive tour work are also undertaken.

Fleet:
Boeing 707
Boeing 737
Fokker F.27

Maersk Air

Formed in 1969 to operate inclusive tour and charter flights from its base at Copenhagen, Maersk Air is a subsidiary of the Moller Shipping Line. Operations began in January 1970 with Fokker F.27s and a Hawker Siddeley 125. In November 1969 the airline took over Falcks Flyvetjenste A/S, and in the process started to operate scheduled flights to Odense, Karup and Skystrup from Copenhagen; further domestic services have since been added using the airline's de Havilland Canada DHC-7s and Boeing 737s. The commuter airline Airbusiness ApS was taken over on 1

Maersk Air (continued)

May 1983; Maersk Air also holds a 38 per cent interest in Danair A/S, which was formed in November 1971 jointly with Scandinavian Airlines System and Cimber Air. Also undertaken by the airline are off-shore operations with its fleet of helicopters.

Fleet:
Aérospatiale Super Puma
Bell 212

Boeing 737
de Havilland Canada DHC-7
Hawker Siddeley 125

Malaysian Airline System

Malaysian Airline System was incorporated under that title in April 1971, although it is a descendant of Malayan Airways which was formed in 1947 by Mansfield and Co. Ltd. In its early days the airline operated Douglas DC-3s, and from 1948 BOAC held an interest in the airline, which was also helped by QANTAS in expanding its network. On 1 August 1959 two Vickers Viscounts were acquired, and for use on long-distance flights Bristol Britannias were also flown, only to be replaced from December 1962 by de Havilland Comet 4s. In November 1962 the airline's title was revised to Malaysian Airways. On 1 November 1967 the airline changed its name to Malaysian Singapore Airlines, and further injection of new equipment soon followed in the shape of Boeing 707s and 737s. From 1 October 1972 the countries of Malaysia and Singapore began operating independently. MAS services to London began in 1974 with Boeing 707s. The airline's first Douglas DC-10-30 was delivered

on 2 August 1976 and more recently, in 1982, the airline acquired two Boeing 747s for its intercontinental flights, which now include destinations in Europe, the Middle East, Australia and throughout the Far East. The airline's domestic and short-haul network uses mainly Boeing 737s, de Havilland Canada DHC-6s and Fokker F.27s.

Fleet:
Airbus A300
Boeing 737
Boeing 747
Britten-Norman Islander
de Havilland Canada DHC-6
Douglas DC-10
Fokker F.27

Malaysian Airline System flies two Boeing 747s on intercontinental flights to Europe, Australia and the Middle East.

Malev

Maszovlet (Magyar Szovjet Legiforgalmi Társaság) was formed by the Soviet Union and Hungary on 29 March 1946, and commenced domestic operations with Lisunov Li-2s on 15 October of the same year. In November 1954 the current name of Magyar Légiköz-lekedési Vállalat (Malev for short) was adopted. In May 1960 the turbo-prop-powered Ilyushin Il-18 entered service, and by then numerous destinations such as Amsterdam, Stockholm and Moscow were being served. In December 1968 the airline introduced its first two Tupolev Tu-134s, and five years later (in September 1973) the first Tupolev Tu-154 entered service. Currently Malev operates passenger and cargo services to points in Europe, the Middle East and North Africa.

Fleet:
Ilyushin Il-18
Tupolev Tu-134
Tupolev Tu-154

The Tupolev Tu-134 provides the cornerstone of Malev's fleet, being used widely throughout Hungary and Europe.

Martinair

Founded on 24 May 1958, Martin Air Charter numbered among its early activities air taxi operations, aerial survey work and joy ride flights. In January 1964 Fairways of Rotterdam was taken over, and later in that year KLM took a 25 per cent interest in the airline and also transferred some of its aircraft to Martin Air Charter, namely Douglas

Martinair operates worldwide charter flights with the Douglas DC-9, DC-10 Series 30 (illustrated) and the Airbus A310.

Martinair (continued)

DC-7Cs and DC-8s. The airline adopted its current name, Martinair, in 1967, the full title being Martin's Luchtvervoer Maatschappij NV. The airline's first wide-body aircraft was a Douglas DC-10-30CF, of which the first example was delivered on 13 November 1973. Martinair now operates worldwide charter services with its fleet of DC-9s and DC-10s plus its latest acquisition, the Airbus A310. Martinair has a subsidiary called Martinair Vesting Vlieveld Lelystad BV, which operates through smaller companies on activities such as flying training, aerial surveys, advertising, sightseeing and business charters.

Fleet:
Airbus A310
Douglas DC-9
Douglas DC-10

Mexicana

Compania Mexicana de Transportes Aereos was formed in 1921, its current name of Mexicana being adopted on 20 August 1924. Scheduled services began on 29 May 1928 between Mexico City and Tampico, and services to the USA started on 10 March 1929. Also in 1929 Pan American Airways bought the airline, this ownership being relinquished in 1968. Jet services started in 1960 with de Havilland Comet 4Cs, followed by Boeing 727s in 1966. The first two of the airline's Douglas DC-10-15s were delivered on 15 June 1981. At present the airline operates Boeing 727s and DC-10-15s on scheduled passenger and cargo flights to 27 points within Mexico, to nine cities in the USA, and

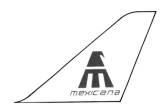

to Havana, San Juan, Guatemala City, San Jose and Costa Rica. On 15 July 1982 the Mexican government became the major shareholder in the airline with a 58 per cent interest.

Fleet:
Boeing 727
Douglas DC-10

Mexicana's Douglas DC-10s are mainly used on scheduled flights to the United States, but also serve cities in the Caribbean.

Middle East Airlines

Established in May 1945, MEA began operations in January 1946 with de Havilland D.H.89A Dragon Rapides; within six months two Douglas DC-3s had been added to the fleet. In 1949 Pan American Airways took a 36 per cent interest in the airline, and supplied aircraft and technical assistance, but this association ended in January 1955. One month later MEA became a subsidiary of BOAC, and this new agreement brought the airline its first Vickers Viscounts in July 1957. The airline's first jet equipment was the de Havilland Comet 4C, of which the first was delivered on 19 December 1960. BOAC's holding in MEA was terminated in August 1961. Towards the end of the 1960s Boeing 707s and 720s replaced the Comets. On 30 May 1975 the Airline's first Boeing 747-B4B was delivered. These aircraft have spent a great deal of time working for other airlines: as a result of Lebanon's internal conflicts large-capacity aircraft have not been needed for MEA's own operations. From its base at Beirut MEA serves destinations in the Middle East, Europe, and North and West Africa. Major shareholders are Intra Investments and Air France.

Fleet:
Boeing 707
Boeing 720
Boeing 747

MEA's Boeing 747 fleet has recently been leased to other airlines as a result of the internal turmoil in Lebanon.

Minerve

The French privately-owned charter airline Minerve (Cie Française de Transports Aériens) was formed on 15 June 1975 with a single Sud-Aviation Caravelle, which started services in November 1975. The airline currently operates Caravelles and Douglas DC-8s on passenger and cargo charters to points in Africa, the Americas, Europe, and the Middle and Far East.

Fleet:
Douglas DC-8

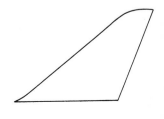

Sud-Aviation Caravelle

Monarch Airlines

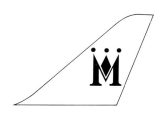

Formed on 5 June 1967 to operate world-wide charters and inclusive tour flights, Monarch Airlines made its first commercial flight on 5 April 1968 using a Bristol Britannia 312. On 15 September 1971 Monarch acquired its first pure jet, a Boeing 720-051B, which entered service on 13 December 1971. On 18 December 1975 the last Britannia service was flown and until October 1980 the airline operated only Boeing 707s and 720s plus BAC One-Elevens. On 1 October 1980 the first Boeing 737 was delivered, being joined on 26 March 1983 by the airline's first Boeing 757. Currently Monarch Airlines operates BAC One-Elevens, and Boeing 737s and 757s on flights from most of the UK airports (excluding Heathrow) to points in Europe, the Middle East and North Africa.

Fleet:
BAC One-Eleven
Boeing 737
Boeing 757

Nigeria Airways

In June 1958 West African Airways Corporation became known as Nigeria Airways (the original airline's history can be traced back to 1946). The new airline was owned by the Nigerian government (51 per cent), Elder Demster (33 per cent) and BOAC (16 per cent), the last providing the aircraft (Boeing Stratocruisers and Bristol Britannias). In March 1961 Nigeria Airways became state owned. Jet services to London started with de Havilland Comet 4s on 1 April 1962. On 17 May 1971 the airline's first owned Boeing 707 was delivered, the new type replacing leased Vickers VC10s on the international services. Currently on its domestic and regional destinations the company uses the Boeing 727 and 737 and the Fokker F.28, whereas on its long-haul flights the Douglas DC-10-30 (first delivered on 14 October 1976) and Airbus A310 are supplemented by the Boeing 707. International services are flown from Lagos, Kano and Port Harcourt to six points in Europe and to New York and Jeddah. The airline also operates to other West African countries, and has a domestic schedule to 19 towns in Nigeria.

Nigeria Airways' long haul routes are handled by the Douglas DC-10. These are supplemented on lower density sectors by the Boeing 707.

Monarch's holiday travel achieved new status when it acquired Boeing 757s, which are used on the longer-haul charter routes.

Nigeria Airways (continued)

Fleet:
Airbus A310
Boeing 707
Boeing 727

Boeing 737
Douglas DC-10
Fokker F.28

NLM City Hopper

A wholly-owned subsidiary of KLM Royal Dutch Airlines, NLM (Nederlandse Luchtvaart Maatschappij) was formed in 1966 to operate Dutch domestic services, which began on 29 August 1966. Initial equipment was the Fokker F.27 Friendships which still constitutes the largest proportion of the airlines's fleet, the balance being Fokker F.28 Fellowships; the first of the twin-jets was delivered on 3 March 1978. In 1975 NLM began international services which now serve Belgium, France, West Germany and the UK.

Fleet:
Fokker F.27
Fokker F.28

Northwest Orient Airlines

The airline was formed on 1 August 1926 as Northwest Airways and operated its first mail flight with a Curtiss Oriole on 1 October 1926. Nine months later, on 1 July 1928, passenger services were started with three Stinson SB-1 Detroiters. International services to Winnipeg were launched in 1931. The airlines' current title, Northwest Orient Airlines, was adopted on 16 April 1934 when the airline was reorganized. On 22 April 1939 the first

Douglas DC-3 was delivered, and between then and 1958 Northwest operated 36 of the type. After the war the airline operated

Northwest Orient operates a large fleet of Douglas DC-10 Series 40 (illustrated) and Boeing 747s across the US, Europe and the Far East.

Northwest Orient Airlines (continued)

10 Boeing 377 Stratocruisers, the first being delivered on 22 June 1949 for initial service on the Honolulu route. The Stratocruisers were replaced by Lockheed L-188 Electras, the first of these turboprop airliners being delivered on 19 July 1959. One year later, on 18 May 1960, the first pure jet, a Douglas DC-8-32, was delivered and Northwest was the first airline to operate the type across the Pacific. The end of April 1970 saw the arrival of the first Boeing 747-151, which began operations on 22 June between New York and Minneapolis/St Paul. Currently the only other wide-body aircraft the airline uses is the Douglas DC-10-40. Northwest Orient Airlines is the second oldest airline in the USA to retain its original corporate name, and has never merged with any other operator. The airline currently operates passenger and cargo flights across the whole of the USA, plus services to the Far East, and to Copenhagen, Glasgow, Hamburg, London, Oslo, Shannon and Stockholm in Europe.

Fleet:
Boeing 727
Boeing 747
Douglas DC-10

Olympic Airways

Established on 1 January 1957 by the Greek shipowner Aristotle Onassis to take over the assets of Greek Airlines TAE, which had been formed in 1951, Olympic Airways began operations with a single Douglas DC-4 and 14 DC-3s on 6 April 1957. On 18 May 1960 jet services from Athens to London were started in conjuction with BEA, using the latter's de Havilland Comet 4Bs. Since that time the airline has operated four different Boeing types, namely the Boeing 707 (first entered service in June 1966), the Boeing 727 (first delivered in December 1968), the Boeing 737 (first delivered on 26 June 1976) and the Boeing 747 (first delivered on 21 June 1973). On 1 January 1975 the airline came under the control of the Greek government when Aristotle Onassis sold his interest in the airline. At present Olympic Airways flies domestic services to 28 cities and islands, and internationally serves over 30 cities throughout Africa, Europe, the Middle and Far East, and North America, plus a service to Sydney and Melbourne in Australia.

First delivered in 1976, Olympic's Boeing 737s get high utilization on short- and medium-haul routes in Europe and within Greece itself.

Olympic Airways (continued)

Fleet:

Airbus A300
Boeing 707
Boeing 727

Boeing 737
Boeing 747
Britten-Norman Islander

Dornier Do 228
Shorts 330
Shorts Skyvan

Orion Airways

Formed by Horizon Travel on 28 November 1978 to operate inclusive tours and charters, Orion Airways started its first services in March 1980 with four Boeing 737s. The company now operates (for its owners and for other tour operators) from most of the major airports in the UK to points in Europe, North Africa and the Mediterranean. The fleet of Boeing 737-200s is shortly to be joined by five Boeing 737-300s, which will be the first delivered to any airline outside the USA.

Fleet:
Boeing 737

Ozark Air Lines

Based at St Louis, Missouri, Ozark Air Lines was formed on 1 September 1943 to carry out interstate and charter services. Its first scheduled service was on 26 September 1950 between St Louis and Chicago with a Douglas DC-3. Over the next decade the airline expanded its operations to include 10 states in the mid-west of the USA. To supplement the DC-3s, Fairchild F-27s were delivered in July 1959 followed by FH-227s in 1966. The airline's initial jet was the Douglas DC-9-15, the first being delivered on 25 May 1966. Ozark Air Lines currently operates Boeing 727s and DC-9s (all the major marks excluding the Series

50) to more than 60 cities in 25 states of the USA.

Fleet:
Boeing 727
Douglas DC-9

Pacific Southwest Airlines

PSA was created as an airline division of Friedkin Aeronautics Inc. in 1945, and was intended to operate charter flights. But in May 1949 domestic services started in California with a leased Douglas DC-3. As a result of the wealth and air-mindedness of the state of California PSA expanded very quickly. In November 1959 the first of five Lockheed L-188 Electras began operations between San Diego, Los Angeles and San Francisco. Early April 1965 saw the delivery of PSA's first jet, a Boeing 727-14. For a brief period, from 1974-78, the airline

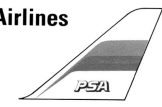

operated a wide-body airliner, the Lockheed L-1011 TriStar. To replace the later Boeing 727-214s, and to allow a greater frequency of service, the airline ordered 20 British Aerospace 146-200s, of which the first two were accepted on 13 June 1984.

From its St Louis, Missouri, base Ozark operates a mixed fleet on domestic routes. Major type is the Douglas DC-9.

Pacific Southwest Airlines (continued)

The airline's fleet now consists of British Aerospace 146s and Douglas DC-9s, which fly a high-frequency low-cost service to 20 cities in five west coast states of the USA.

Fleet:
British Aerospace 146
Douglas DC-9

Pacific Western Airlines

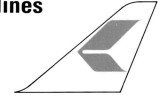

Based at Vancouver in British Columbia, Pacific Western Airlines was founded on 1 April 1945 as Central British Columbia Airways to operate charter services. During the 1950s many smaller operators were taken over, and as a consequence PWA started services to north and west Canada. On 3 November 1967 the airline began to operate the Boeing 707-138B on international charters, and in the same year Lockheed L-100-20s were bought to undertake cargo charters. The majority of the airline's services are carried out by the Boeing 737, of which the first was delivered on 26 November 1968, assisted by the Boeing 767 on the high-density routes throughout British Columbia, Alberta, Saskatchewan, Manitoba, The Northwest Territories and Yukon. International passenger and cargo charters are also undertaken.

Fleet:
Boeing 737

Boeing 767
Lockheed L-100

Pakistan International Airlines

Formed by the Pakistani government on 11 March 1955, Pakistan International Airlines (which had been operating from 7 June 1954, prior to its official foundation) resulted from the reorganization of Orient Airways, which had been formed on 23 October 1940. International routes to Cairo and London were started on 1 February 1955, operated by Lockheed L-1049C Super Constellations. To help modernize

Pakistan International Airlines now employs both the Boeing 747 and the Douglas DC-10 (illustrated) on its international routes.

Pakistan International Airlines (continued)

the domestic fleet of Convair CV-240s and Douglas DC-3s, Vickers Viscounts were ordered, the first of the turboprop airliners being handed over on 2 January 1959, and being followed by Fokker F.27 Friendships from January 1961. PIA has the distinction of being the first Asian airline to introduce a pure jet, a leased Boeing 707-121 operating the London service on 7 March 1960. To replace the Viscounts four Hawker Siddeley Tridents were ordered, the first delivered on 1 March 1966 remaining in service until 1970. Pakistan International's first wide-body aircraft was the Douglas DC-10-30, of which the first was delivered on 1 March 1974. With the Boeing 747s these operate

the majority of the airline's long-haul inter-continental flights, assisted by the Boeing 707. On the domestic and regional services the Airbus A300 and Fokker F.27 are the two main types. PIA currently operates scheduled passenger and cargo flights throughout the Far East, Europe, North Africa and the USA.

Fleet:
Airbus A300
Boeing 707
Boeing 720
Boeing 747
Douglas DC-10
Fokker F.27

Pan American World Airways

One of the world's major airlines, Pan American was established on 14 March 1927 by Juan Terry Trippe. A Fokker F.VII trimotor operated the airline's first mail service on 28 October 1927, and passenger services followed on 16 January of the following year. By the end of 1929 the airline had flights to 23 countries in Latin America. In 1931 Pan American operated the first commercial four-engine flying-boat, the Sikorsky S-40 which it named *American Clipper,* and from that time all Pan American multi-engine aircraft have borne the 'Clipper' name. Transpacific and trans-atlantic services were started on 22 November 1935 and 20 May 1939 respectively, using Martin 130s on the former and

Boeing 314s on the latter. During World War II Pan American helped to establish many airports in Africa and Asia, and with the Douglas DC-4 carried out military transport missions throughout these continents. After the war Pan American helped form new Asian airlines, such as THY and Iran Air, plus many more in Southern and Central America. In 1950 Pan American Airways changed its name to Pan American

Pan Am's latest acquisitions are Airbus products, the A300 (illustrated) and the A310, used for medium-haul international routes.

Pan American World Airways (continued)

World Airways and the same year acquired American Overseas Airlines. On 13 October 1955 the carrier announced it was buying 45 US-built jet aircraft, namely the Boeing 707 and Douglas DC-8; the first of the former was delivered on 20 October 1958. Working with Boeing, Pan American helped to create the Boeing 747 and on 22 January 1970 the first of these wide-bodied airliners operated its first service between New York and London. On 22 December 1979 Pan American took over National Airlines: on 7 January 1980 National became a full subsidiary, and was finally integrated on 26 October. And so in the space of just over 50 years Pan Am (as it is now commonly known) has grown from a small mail carrier to one of the world's largest airlines operating services throughout the world, plus US domestic services and flights within Germany, including West Berlin. On the airline's international services the Boeing 747 is the primary equipment, supplemented by Airbus A300 and A310s plus Douglas DC-10s, whereas on the domestic services in the USA the Boeing 727 is operated in addition to the wide-bodied aircraft, and in Germany Pan Am uses Boeing 737s.

Fleet:
Airbus A300
Airbus A310
Boeing 727
Boeing 737
Boeing 747
Douglas DC-10
Lockheed L-1011 TriStar

People Express

In the early spring of 1980 former Texas International Airlines president, D. C. Burr, and other ex-TIA executives founded People Express. Operations began on 30 April 1981 with ex-Lufthansa Boeing 737-100s on high-density low-cost services from a base at Newark, New Jersey to points in the eastern States of the USA. Since that time there has been a considerable increase in the airline's fleet, which now includes also Boeing 747s and Boeing 727s. In the summer of 1983 People

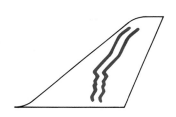

Express started a low-cost no-frills service across the Atlantic between Newark and London Gatwick using Boeing 747s.

Fleet:
Boeing 727

Boeing 737
Boeing 747

Philippine Air Lines

Re-formed on 25 February 1941 as Philippine Air Lines, the new airline took over from Philippine Air Transport which had ceased operations in July 1940. After the invasion by the Japanese in December 1941 no further flights were made until 14 February 1946, when with five Douglas DC-3s the airline resumed domestic flights, switching to leased Douglas DC-4s on 31 July 1946. Trooping charters to Oakland, California were started on 29 May 1948. Using a Douglas DC-6 the airline started its first round-the-world flights, one of the ports of call being London. So in two years Philippine Air Lines (PAL) had graduated

from a domestic operator to fully fledged international carrier. On 10 May 1957 the airline's first Vickers Viscount was delivered for use mainly on the domestic schedule. Further modernization of the domestic fleet took place in 1960 when the Fokker F.27 entered service, being superseded by the Hawker Siddeley 748 in 1967.

Philippine Air Lines (continued)

Short- and medium-range flights are handled by the Airbus A300.

PAL's first pure jet aircraft was a leased Pan American Boeing 707, which operated in 1962, but this type was soon replaced by leased KLM Douglas DC-8s on 20 June of the same year. To update the domestic fleet further and to replace the Viscounts another UK-built aircraft was purchased, namely the BAC One-Eleven 500; the first of these was delivered on 19 April 1966. Two wide-body types are used on PAL's high-density long-haul flights, namely the Douglas DC-10-30 (first leased on 11 July 1974) and the Boeing 747 (first delivered on 21 December 1979). On the short- and medium-distance flights the Airbus A300,

BAC One-Eleven, Boeing 727 and Hawker Siddeley 748 are mainly used. PAL currently operates to 28 international destinations in the Middle and Far East, Europe and the USA, and to 40 points within the Philippines.

Fleet:
Airbus A300
Boeing 727
Boeing 747
BAC One-Eleven
Douglas DC-10
Hawker Siddeley 748

Piedmont Air Lines

Piedmont Aviation was established as a charter and general aviation company on 2 July 1940. The airline division was formed on 1 January 1948 and began operations with Douglas DC-3s on 20 February 1948. Fairchild F-27s were introduced to the network in mid-November 1958, and these were replaced by the larger FH-227 in 1966. In March 1967 Piedmont Air Lines leased its first jets, namely Boeing 727s, but these were soon replaced by Boeing 737s, the first of these twin-jets being delivered on 30 May 1968. But since that time the Boeing 727 has rejoined the fleet (in December 1976) and with the Model 737s and Fokker F.28 Fellowships the airline operates ser-

vices throughout the north, east and midwest of the USA.

Fleet:
Boeing 727
Boeing 737
Fokker F.28

Qantas

Queensland and Northern Territory Aerial Services (QANTAS) was formed on 1

November 1920; it was known as Qantas Empire Airways from 18 January 1934 and

Qantas (continued)

on 1 August 1967 adopted its present title of Qantas Airways. Initially the airline operated services within Australia, but on 18 January 1934, in conjunction with Imperial Airways, Qantas started to operate a service to Singapore. On 31 May 1945, and using Avro Lancastrians, the airline flew its first service to London. On 1 April 1959 the first jet entered service, a Boeing 707-138B, eventually replacing the Lockheed L-1049G Super Constellations which had been operated since April 1954. The airline currently operates only the Boeing 747 (first delivered on 30 July 1971), on all its routes to New Zealand, the Far East, North America, Europe and Africa, but very shortly the Boeing 767 will take over some of the Asian routes.

Fleet:
Boeing 747

Qantas operates an all-Boeing 747 fleet. These are used for long-haul international flights throughout the world.

Republic Air Lines

Republic Air Lines evolved from the merger of North Central Airlines (formed 15 May 1944) and Southern Airways (formed July 1943) on 1 July 1979. Services began under the new name on 1 October 1979 serving a comprehensive network of US routes through the central states plus Mexico, the Cayman Islands and Thunder Bay. On 1 October 1980 Republic took over Hughes Airwest, and as a result of this transaction the airline currently flies a network of scheduled passenger and cargo flights linking more than 140 cities in 29 states, plus international services to Canada, Mexico and Grand Cayman. The airline has a large fleet of Douglas DC-9s (135 approximately)

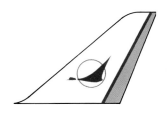

plus Boeing 727s and Convair CV-580s.

Fleet:
Boeing 727
Convair CV-580
Douglas DC-9

Royal Air Maroc

The Moroccan state airline, Royal Air Maroc, can trace its history back to 9 October 1946 when the Société Air Atlas was formed. On 28 June 1953 SAA merged

Royal Air Maroc (continued)

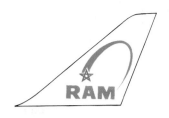

with Avia Maroc Aérienne (founded in 1947) to form the Compagnie Chérifienne de Transport Aérien (CCTA). The new airline initially operated domestic services and a limited number of flights to Europe. After Morocco gained its independence CCTA changed its name on 28 June 1957 to Royal Air Maroc. In that year the first Lockheed L-749A Constellation was delivered for use on the airline's international services. On 19 July 1958, the first jet was delivered, a Sud-Aviation Caravelle IA, and with this type further European services were added. In May 1970 the Boeing 727-2D6 started to replace the Caravelles. On the airline's long-haul services, such as those to North and South America, Royal Air Maroc uses its Boeing 707s and single Boeing 747,

whereas on the airline's domestic, North African and European services the Boeing 727 and 737 are mainly used.

Fleet:
Boeing 707
Boeing 727
Boeing 737
Boeing 747

Royal Air Maroc flies an all-Boeing fleet throughout the Middle East, North Africa and Europe. Illustrated is a Boeing 737.

SABENA

The Société Anonyme Belge d'Exploitation de la Navigation Aérienne (SABENA) was formed by business interests in Belgium and the Congo on 23 May 1923. During the 1920s services within Europe and the Belgian Congo were started. During World War II SABENA suspended its European services but continued operating in Africa. Transatlantic services started on 4 June 1947 with Douglas DC-4s operating between Brussels and New York. The airline's first jet-powered aircraft was the Boeing 707-329, which began services between Brussels and New York on 23 January 1960. On 28 January 1960 SABENA ceased internal African services when Air Congo (now Air Zaïre) came into existence. On 20 January 1961 the Sud-Aviation Caravelle was delivered to the airline, this rear-

engined twin-jet being bought to replace the piston-engined Convair CV-440. For its long-haul services SABENA currently uses the Boeing 747-129 (first delivered 19 November 1970) and the Douglas DC-10-30 (first delivered 18 September 1973) on the airline's European and Middle East services the Airbus A310 and Boeing 737 are mainly used. Currently SABENA operates a far-reaching network of passenger and cargo flights within Europe and to the Middle and

SABENA (continued)

Far East, Africa and North America.

The Airbus A310 is SABENA's latest acquisition and is used alongside Boeing 737s on routes throughout Europe and the Middle East.

Fleet:
Airbus A310
Boeing 737
Boeing 747
Douglas DC-10

Saudia

Saudi Arabian Airlines was established in May 1945 with a small fleet of Douglas DC-3s, and scheduled passenger services started on 14 March 1947. The airline remained a domestic carrier until late in 1961, when services to neighbouring Middle East countries started. On 20 December 1961 the airline's first jet aircraft was delivered, a Boeing 720-068B, soon introduced on the new international services, and in January 1968 Saudi Arabian Airlines began operating to London. In 1972 the airline adopted the name Saudia, and on 14 March 1972 the first Boeing 737 was delivered, and introduced on the domestic and regional services as a replacement for the Convair CV-340 and Douglas DC-9. June 1975 saw the delivery of the carrier's first wide-body aircraft, a Lockheed L-1011 TriStar 1, which helped expand the airline's network. To cater for the phenomenal increase in passenger demand two Boeing 747s were leased from Middle East Airlines on 1 June 1977, and subsequently Saudia bought its own Boeing 747s, the first delivered on 24 April 1981. The carrier now operates an

extensive domestic network to 20 destinations (mainly with Boeing 737s and Airbus A300s) and international services to Europe, the Middle East, Africa and North America (mainly with Airbus A300s, Boeing 747s and Lockheed TriStars). All-freight services with Douglas DC-8s are also undertaken.

Fleet:
Airbus A300
Boeing 707
Boeing 737
Boeing 747
Douglas DC-8
Fokker F.28
Lockheed L-1011 TriStar

Scandinavian Airlines System

Scandinavian Airlines System was created on 31 July 1946 by the merging of the

national airlines of Denmark, Norway and Sweden, respectively Det Danske Luftfart-

Boeing 747SPs fly Saudia's prestige
routes alongside regular Boeing 747s and
Lockheed TriStars.

Scandinavian Airlines System (continued)

selskab (DDL), Det Norske Luftfartselskap (DNL) and AB Aerotransport (ABA of Sweden), all of which had been founded in the 1920s. The airline was formed primarily to serve Europe and across the North Atlantic, and it was not until 1954 that the three airlines operated under the one name. During the early 1950s services to South American and South Africa were started with Douglas DC-6s. The first jet airliner, was delivered on 1 April 1959, a Sud-Aviation Caravelle, this French-built jet being replaced later by the Douglas DC-9. This currently constitutes the largest part of the SAS fleet and is used with the Airbus A300 on the European network. Like many other carriers SAS was quick to order the Boeing 747; the first of these wide-body airliners was delivered on 22 February 1971, and with this type and the Douglas DC-10-30 the airline operates its long-haul services to

Africa, the Middle and Far East and the Americas. Airlines in which SAS has an interest are Scanair (100 per cent) Danair A/S (57 per cent), Linjeflyg (50 per cent), Greenlandair (25 per cent) and Wideroes (22 per cent).

Fleet:
Airbus A300
Boeing 747
Douglas DC-8
Douglas DC-9
Douglas DC-10
Fokker F.27

SAS's new livery reflects the multi-national nature of the airline. The coloured bands around the lower fuselage represent the flags of Sweden, Norway and Denmark.

Singapore Airlines

Formed as Malayan Airways, the airline began domestic operations on 1 May 1947 and international services in 1948. With the help of BOAC, international services were expanded and turboprop Bristol Britannias were leased from the British airline in September 1961, followed by de Havilland Comet 4s in late 1965. On 30 December 1966 the name was changed to Malaysian-Singapore Airlines and operations continued under this title until 1 October 1972, when the two countries formed their own airlines. On 31 July 1973 Singapore Airlines took delivery of its first Boeing 747-212B, and together with the Douglas DC-10-30s

they form the backbone of the airline's long-haul fleet to destinations in Europe, the Middle East, the USA and Australia. On its short-haul destinations the airline operates the Boeing 757 and 727, plus Airbus A300s and A310s to points throughout the Far East.

Douglas DC-10s form the backbone of Singapore's medium-haul routes, whilst a large fleet of Boeing 747s operates the long-haul routes.

Singapore Airlines (continued)

Fleet:

Airbus A300	Boeing 747
Airbus A310	Boeing 757
Boeing 727	Douglas DC-10

Sobelair

The Belgian charter operator Société Belge de Transportation par Air SA (Sobelair) was established on 30 July 1946 and began operations from Belgium to the Congo in that same year. In 1947 the airline supplemented SABENA on its operations in the Belgian Congo; the latter airline took a majority holding in Sobelair in 1948. The airline's first jets were ex-SABENA Sud-Aviation Caravelles, the first three of which were delivered on 31 March 1971. Currently this non-IATA subsidiary of SABENA operates a fleet of one Boeing 707 and three Boeing 737s, mainly on inclusive tour and charter flights within Europe plus, on occasion, flights for SABENA.

Fleet:
Boeing 707
Boeing 737

South African Airways

Union Airways, formed in August 1929, was acquired by the government-owned South African Railways and Harbours Administration on 1 February 1934 and was then named South African Airways. Until 10 November 1944 the airline operated only domestic services, but from that date services to London were started with leased Avro Yorks. The first pressurized airliner used by South African Airways was the Lockheed L-749A Constellation, the first of the type being delivered on 24 April 1950 and went into service on the European

South African Airways flies the Boeing 747 on long-haul routes, and has recently adopted the stretched upper deck 747-300 version.

South African Airways (continued)

destinations replacing Douglas DC-4s. For a short time at the end of 1952 and in early 1953 South African Airways operated a leased de Havilland Comet IA. The domestic and regional services were modernized by the introduction of the Vickers Viscount, the first two being delivered on 26 October 1958. On 1 October 1960 the Boeing 707 started to replace Douglas DC-7Bs on the London services. The airline's first wide-body airliner, the Boeing 747, was delivered on 22 October 1971 and (with the 747SP) operates its long-haul routes to Europe, Australia and North and South America. On domestic and regional services the Airbus A300 and Boeing 737s are operated.

Fleet:
Airbus A300
Boeing 737
Boeing 747

Southwest Airlines

Air Southwest was incorporated on 15 March 1967 to operate low-fare one-class scheduled services within the state of Texas. The current title, Southwest Airlines, was adopted on 29 March 1971. The airline began operations on 18 June 1971 with Boeing 737-2H4s, and to the present has owned only this twin-jet type, though it should be noted that Boeing 727s are leased on occasion. Currently Southwest operates flights within Texas and to the neighbouring states of Louisiana, Oklahoma, Arizona, Nevada, Colorado, Missouri, California and New Mexico with its fleet of Boeing 737-200s and leased Boeing 727s.

Fleet:
Boeing 737

Spantax

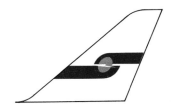

Spanish Taxis (Spantax) was formed on 6 October 1959 with Douglas DC-3s, initially to operate in support of oil and mineral prospecting in the Spanish Sahara. Inclusive tour work began in 1960. Until the late 1960s the airline operated mainly Douglas DC-4s and DC-7s, but on 19 February 1967 its first jet was delivered, a Convair CV-990. In 1972 transatlantic charters began, and an extensive European network was started. The airline's first wide-body airliner, a Douglas DC-10-30, was delivered on 24 October 1978. Charter and inclusive tour work is undertaken to destinations in Europe, Africa, and North and South America with a mixed fleet of jet aircraft.

Fleet:
Boeing 737
Convair CV-990
Douglas DC-8
Douglas DC-9
Douglas DC-10

Sterling Airways

Tjaereborg Rejser A/S, a leading Scandinavian Travel agency, formed Sterling Airways in May 1962. Currently Sterling operates a fleet of Boeing 727s, Douglas DC-8s and Caravelles on flights to Europe, North Africa, North Amierca and Sri Lanka.

Sterling Airways (continued)

The Caravelle was the airline's first jet aircraft.

Fleet:
Boeing 727
Douglas DC-8
Sud-Aviation Caravelle

Sudan Airways

The formation of the state-owned Sudan Airways took place in February 1946, technical and flying assistance being given by the British company Airwork Limited. Domestic services began in July 1947 with four de Havilland D.H.104 Dove 1s and in November 1954 international services began with Douglas DC-3s operating from Khartoum to Cairo. The airline's first turboprop airliner was the Vickers Viscount, which began service to London via Rome on 8 June 1959. On 25 January 1962 the airline's first Fokker F.27 was delivered for use on the domestic and regional network; this 36-seat turboprop airliner replaced the Doves and eventually the DC-3s. On 13 November 1962 the first de Havilland Comet 4C was delivered, but in 1974 the Comets were replaced, initially with leased British Midland Airways Boeing 707s. Now

Sudan Airways' own Boeing 707s operate services to the Middle East, Europe and North Africa, while Boeing 737s and F.27s operate domestic and regional services. For use on its international network Sudan Airways intends to operate three Airbus A310s in the near future.

Fleet:
Boeing 707
Boeing 737
de Havilland Canada DHC-6
Fokker F.27

Swissair

On 26 March 1931 Balair (Basler Luftverkehr) and Ad Astra Aero AG merged to form Swissair (Schweizerische Luftverkehr AG). In early 1935 Douglas DC-2s entered service with the airline, allowing the start of services to London on 1 April, and DC-3s were delivered in 1937. World War II stopped operations, but on 16 July 1945 European services were resumed. In February 1947 Swissair took over Alpar Bern, and so became the official state airline. On 29 April 1947 a Douglas DC-4 service to New York started. The airline's first jet aircraft, a Sud-Aviation Caravelle, entered service on 21 April 1960 between Zurich and London, followed nine days later by the Douglas DC-8 on the New York route. A Boeing 747, the airline's first widebody aircraft was delivered on 29 January 1971, and with the Douglas DC-10-30 (first entered service in December 1972) Swissair operates the majority of its long-haul

flights to the Middle and Far East, Africa, and North and South America. On its shorthaul network the airline uses its newly acquired Airbus A310s and Douglas DC-9s. Aviation-orientated associate companies include Balair, CTA, and Swissair Photo and Surveys. Currently the airline is owned 75 per cent by private investors and 25 per cent by public institutions.

Fleet:
Airbus A310
Boeing 747
Douglas DC-9
Douglas DC-10

Swissair has operated DC-9s for many years in several marks and now uses the latest Series 80 aircraft on its European routes.

Syrian Air

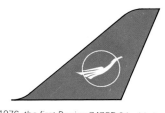

Formed in October 1961 to succeed Syrian Airways (established on 22 December 1946), Syrianair (Syrian Arab Airlines) started life with three Douglas DC-6Bs inherited from United Arab Airlines (February 1958 to September 1961). In 1964 international services were started with flights to Paris and London, and through the Gulf states to Karachi and Delhi. On 27 October 1965 the airline's first jet was delivered a Sud-Aviation Caravelle 10B. Just over 10 years later, on 21 May 1976, the first Boeing 747SP-94 wide-body airliner was delivered, and this is used mainly on the airline's services to Europe, Asia and Africa, whereas on the domestic and regional services the Boeing 727 and various Soviet types are operated.

Fleet:
Boeing 727
Boeing 747
Ilyushin Il-76
Tupolev Tu-134
Yakovlev Yak-40

Syria's internal routes, and those to neighbouring Arab countries, are handled by Syrian Air's fleet of Boeing 727s.

TAAG Angola Airlines

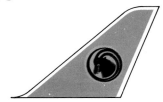

TAAG Angola Airlines was formed originally as Direcçao de Exploraçao dos Transportes Aéreos (DTA) in September 1938 to operate domestic services with de Havilland D.H.89A Dragon Rapides. On 17 July 1940 scheduled domestic services commenced. The airline's current title was adopted on 1 October 1973. TAAG operates an extensive domestic network with Boeing 737s (first delivered 19 November 1975), Fokker F.27s, Yakovlev Yak-40s and Antonov An-26s, whereas on its international services within Africa and to Europe it uses mainly Boeing 707s plus two Lockheed L-100-20 Hercules for all-cargo flights.

Fleet:
Antonov An-26
Boeing 707
Fokker F.27
Lockheed L-100
Yakovlev Yak-40

TAP/Air Portugal

Transportes Aéreos Portugueses SARL (TAP for short) was formed by the Portuguese civil aeronautic secretariat in 1944. The newly formed airline operated its inaugural flight from Lisbon to Madrid with a Douglas DC-3 on 19 September 1946. Further European destinations were added in 1947, plus services to Laurenco Marques via Luanda. In 1953 the airline was sold to private interests, only to be renationalized in April 1975. In 1960 a pooling agreement with BEA meant that the airline started to operate Vickers Viscounts and de Havilland Comet 4Bs. This contract ended when TAP took delivery of its first jet, a Sud-Aviation Caravelle VIR, on 13 July 1962. In June 1966 Boeing 707 services were started to Rio de Janeiro. The airline's first wide-body airliner was the Boeing 747-282B, which was delivered on 20 December 1971. In March 1979 the airline chose its new title of TAP/Air Portugal, and at the same time adopted its current colour scheme. Air Portugal operates an extensive network of passenger and cargo routes within Europe, mainly with Boeing 727s and 737s, and on flights to Africa and to North and South America it uses Lockheed L-1011 TriStar 500s; the first of these wide-body aircraft was delivered on 12 January 1983. The TriStars are at present assisted by the airline's now dwindling fleet of Boeing 707s.

Fleet:

Boeing 707
Boeing 727
Boeing 737
de Havilland Canada DHC-6
Lockheed L-1011 TriStar

TAP flies the long-range Lockheed TriStar 500 to destinations in North and South America and Africa.

TAROM

In 1946 Transporturi Aeriene Romana Sovietica (TARS) was formed as a joint Romanian/Soviet airline to take over from the pre-war state airline called LARS. In 1954 the airline took up its present title of Transporturile Aeriene Romane (TAROM) and at the same time was taken over completely by the Romanian government. In the mid-1950s Ilyushin Il-14s were delivered, enabling the airline to expand its European operations, and in the early 1960s the turbo-

TAROM (continued)

TAROM's major overseas type is the Ilyushin Il-62, and these are regular visitors at European airports, New York and Moscow.

prop-powered Ilyushin Il-18 became soon the backbone of the airline's fleet. On 14 June 1968 the first BAC One-Eleven was received, and this type took over most of the European services until the advent of the Tupolev Tu-154 in 1976. On long-haul flights TAROM uses Boeing 707s (first delivered in February 1974) and Ilyushin Il-62s (delivered in 1973). The airline currently operates international flights to Europe, Africa, the Middle and Far East, and New York, plus a domestic network. Linile Aeriene Romane (a TAROM subsidiary) was formed in December 1975 to under-take charters and inclusive tours with a fleet of BAC One-Eleven 400s to points in the Mediterranean, Europe and the Balkans.

Fleet:
Antonov An-24
Antonov An-26
BAC One-Eleven
Boeing 707
Ilyushin Il-18
Ilyushin Il-62
Tupolev Tu-154

Thai Airways International

On 14 December 1959 an agreement between the Thai government and Scandinavian Airlines System formed Thai Airways International as the international subsidiary of Thai Airways. On 7 may 1960 services commenced with two leased SAS Douglas DC-6Bs. As a result of heavy competition on the Bangkok-Tokyo route, Thai introduced its first jet equipment, a leased SAS Convair CV-990, on 18 May 1962. During the late 1960s and early 1970s the airline used Douglas DC-8s and Douglas DC-9s on its services. The great expansion, due mainly to tourism, meant that in its first 10 years Thai had become the third largest regional operator in the Far East. The first wide-body aircraft operated by Thai was a leased UTA Douglas DC-10-30 which entered service on 30 May 1975. This was also the first aircraft to appear in the airline's current colour scheme. At present Thai Airways International operates mainly DC-

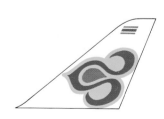

10s and Boeing 747s on its long-haul services to the Middle East, Australia, Europe and USA, while on its Far East services it uses Airbus A300s.

Fleet:
Airbus A300
Boeing 747
Douglas DC-10

Airbus A300s are employed on Far East routes, whilst long-haul services are flown by Boeing 747s and Douglas DC-10s.

TOA Domestic

TOA Domestic was formed on 15 May 1971 by the merger of Japan Domestic Airways and TOA Airways. The airline currently operates an extensive domestic network serving 35 cities within Japan with a fleet of Airbus A300s (first delivered 2 October 1980), of Douglas DC-9s and NAMC YS-11As, plus a varied fleet of helicopters. Japan Air Commuter was established as a wholly-owned subsidiary in 1984 and operates Dornier Do-228-200s.

Fleet:
Airbus A300
Douglas DC-9
NAMC YS-11A

Transport Aérien Transregional

Michel Marchais formed TAT as an airtaxi operation with Beechcraft King Airs in 1968, and scheduled flights commenced in March 1969. On 16 February 1973 the first Fokker F.27 Friendship was delivered, and since that time a large fleet of stretched Fairchild FH-227s has been acquired, together with Fokker F.28 Fellowships. Since TAT's formation many smaller French airlines have been taken over, namely Rousseau Aviation, Taxi Avia France, Paris Air, Air Alpes and Air Alsace. With these acquisitions TAT has now a vast network of routes within France, and more limited international flights (to Germany, Switzerland and the UK) are undertaken. In 1984 the airline changed its name to Transport Aérien Transregional from the previous Touraine Air Transport.

Fleet:
Beechcraft 65 King Air
Beechcraft 99
King Air

Cessna 310
Fairchild/Fokker F-27/F.27
Fairchild FH-227
Fokker F.28

Transamerica

On 20 December 1948 Los Angeles Air Services was formed, and initially this operated Douglas DC-3s on charter flights from a base at Los Angeles. On 18 July 1960 the airline's name was changed to Trans International Airlines, and through the early 1960s this operated Lockheed L-1049 Super Constellations and Douglas DC-8s; the first jet was delivered on 20 June 1962, followed on 30 November by the airline's first DC-8-61. TIA's first Douglas DC-10-30 was delivered on 27 April 1973, and the type was employed mainly on worldwide charter work. On 1 December 1976 TIA took over the supplemental and charter operator Saturn Airways, together with its fleet of Lockheed L-188 Electras and L-100-30 Hercules. On 1 October 1979 the airline's title changed once again to Transamerica Airlines. Since that time the Douglas DC-10-30s have been replaced by Boeing 747s, and currently the airline operates worldwide passenger charters with its fleet of Boeing 747s and Douglas DC-8-73s. On all-cargo work it operates L-100-30s.

Fleet:
Boeing 747
Douglas DC-8
Lockheed L-100

Transamerica (continued)

Transamerica's Boeing 747s are operated on charters around the world. These are also used on US military charters to augment USAF airlift capability.

Trans Australia Airlines

The state-owned Australian domestic carrier Trans Australia Airlines commenced trial operations on 9 September 1946 between Melbourne and Sydney. Regular flights began on 7 October 1946 with 11 war-surplus Douglas DC-3s, later supplemented by four Douglas DC-4s. TAA was one of the earliest operators of the Vickers Viscount, the type entering service on 18 December 1954. On 1 September 1960 TAA took over the QANTAS routes to Papua/New Guinea. Jet operations began on 2 November 1964 when the first Boeing 727-76 entered service. The first wide-body airliner, an Airbus A300, was delivered on 29 June 1981, and with Boeing 727s, Douglas DC-9s and Fokker F.27s these

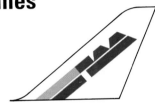

operate passenger and cargo services to over 50 destinations throughout Australia.

Fleet:
Airbus A300
Boeing 727
Fokker F.27
Douglas DC-9

Trans Australia Airlines' only wide-body at present is the Airbus A300, which it uses on high-density sectors around Australia.

Transavia Holland

Founded in 1965 as Transavia (Limburg) NV, the airline commenced charter and inclusive tour operations with three Douglas DC-6Bs on 17 November 1966. The airline's current name, Transavia Holland, was adopted in 1967. Transavia's first jet was delivered on 11 February 1969, a Sud-Aviation Caravelle, and its first Boeing 737 arrived on 17 May 1974. The airline is wholly owned by the Royal Nedlloyd Group. The present fleet of Boeing 737s is used for inclusive tour and charter flights throughout Europe and North Africa. Transavia also carries out work for other airlines throughout the world.

Fleet:
Boeing 737

Transbrasil

On 5 January 1955 SADIA SA Transportes Aéreos (as Transbrasil was then known) began meat haulage operations with a single Douglas DC-3. But from 15 March 1956 passenger flights were undertaken from the airline's base at Sao Paulo to points in the state of Catarina. The first turboprop aircraft operated by SADIA was a leased Handley Page Herald delivered on 6 December 1963. Eventually seven Heralds were used by the airline, the type being superseded by the BAC One-Eleven from September 1970. In June 1972 the current title Transbrasil S/A Linhas Aéreas was adopted. The airline operates Boeing 727s (first two delivered on 2 October 1974) and Boeing 767s (first delivered on 23 June 1983) on services from Brasilia to points in north and south east Brazil, plus international flights to Miami in Florida.

Fleet:
Boeing 727
Boeing 767

Transbrasil flies a large domestic network with Boeing 727s and 767s. The latter also operate to the United States.

Trans European Airways

Established in October 1970 as a charter and inclusive tour carrier from its base at Brussels, Trans European Airways began operations in early 1971 with an ex-Eastern Air Lines Boeing 720-025. In 1973 three Boeing 707-131s were added, and a year later, on 27 November, an Airbus A300 was delivered. At present TEA mainly operates Boeing 737s on European inclusive tour work, supplemented by its Boeing 707s and Airbus A300, and periodically leases out its aircraft to other airlines.

Fleet:
Airbus A300
Boeing 707
Boeing 737

Trans Mediterranean Airways

Formed in 1953 with two Avro York freighters, Trans Mediterranean Airways at first operated non-scheduled cargo services in the Middle East. In October 1959 the airline was redesignated as an international scheduled cargo carrier, and in that year purchased its first Douglas DC-4. In 1966 a leased World Airways Boeing 707-331C began operations for the airline, and at present the Boeing 707 is the sole type the airline operates on its services to the Middle and Far East and Europe. For a short

period (May 1975 to June 1977) TMA operated all-freight configured Boeing 747s.

Fleet:
Boeing 707

Trans Mediterranean Airways is a Lebanon-based all-cargo airline. The Boeing 707 is the sole type used at present, but Boeing 747s were previously operated.

Trans World Airlines

TWA's origins stem from the formation of the mail service operator Western Air Express in 1926. WAE then merged with Transcontinental Air Transport and became

Trans World Airlines (continued)

Transcontinental and Western Air (TWA). In 1934 WAE separated from TWA and later became Western Airlines. In 1930 TWA approached Douglas Aircraft to build the aircraft that eventually became the DC-3. This aircraft, which revolutionized the air transport world, was delivered to TWA in June 1937. On 5 February 1946 the airline inaugurated its international services with flights from New York to Paris operated by a Lockheed L-049 Constellation. On 17 May 1950 the current title (Trans World Airlines) was adopted as the corporate name. The carrier's first jet service was operated between New York and Los Angeles on 20 March 1959 by a Boeing 707-131. Just over 10 years later, on 31 December 1969, the first Boeing 747-131 was delivered, and together with the Lockheed L-1011 Tristar these types currently operate TWA's long-haul routes, which include destinations in Europe and the Middle East. In addition to the wide-body aircraft mentioned, TWA operates Boeing 727s and 767s, plus Douglas DC-9s on a vast domestic network which includes more than 50 cities in the USA.

Fleet:
Boeing 727
Boeing 747
Boeing 767
Douglas DC-9
Lockheed L-1011 TriStar

Better known for its international services, TWA also operates a massive domestic network, utilizing the Douglas DC-9 on many routes.

Tunis Air

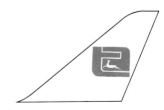

Société Tunisienne de l'Air (Tunis Air) was formed in 1948 by the Tunisian government and Air France and in 1949 began scheduled services with four Douglas DC-3s. Gradually the airline expanded, and in August 1954 with a leased Air France Douglas DC-4 it began flights to Paris. On 31 August 1961 the first Sud-Aviation Caravelle III was delivered, and this type remained with the airline until 1977, by which time the airline had been operating Boeing 727s for five years. Tunis Air operates Boeing 727s and 737s plus an Airbus A300 (delivered on 22 May 1982) on domestic services, plus international flights to the Middle East, North Africa and Europe.

Fleet:
Airbus A300
Boeing 727
Boeing 737

Turk Hava Yollari (THY)

The Turkish state airline was formed on 20 May 1933 as Turkiye Devlet Hava Yollari (Turkish State Airlines). DHY's first route was from Istanbul to Ankara. After World War II DHY had a sizeable fleet of Douglas DC-3s, later joined by de Havilland D.H.114 Heron 2Bs. On 1 March 1956 the airline ceased to exist, being replaced by the current THY (Turk Hava Yollari Ao) airline in which the government had a majority shareholding. Vickers Viscounts were ordered in July 1957, the first arriving on 21 January 1958, but the type was not seen on Western European routes until 1964 when services to Brussels were inaugurated. The first pure jet operated by THY was the Douglas DC-9-14, leased from the manufacturer in August 1967. On 1 December 1972 the airline's first wide-body aircraft was handed over, namely a Douglas DC-10-10. Very recently THY ordered seven Airbus A310s: the first four will be delivered in 1985 and will replace some of the Boeing 707s and 727s currently operated. Used on the airline's services to Europe and the Middle East are the Boeing 707 and 727, and the Douglas DC-9 and DC-10. An extensive domestic network is also operated, mainly by DC-9s, Fokker F.28 Fellowships and de Havilland Canada DHC-7s.

Fleet:
Boeing 707
Boeing 727
de Havilland Canada DHC-7
Douglas DC-9
Douglas DC-10
Fokker F.28

Turk Hava Yollari sustains a European network with the Boeing 727 and Douglas DC-9. These will be supplemented by the Airbus A310.

United Airlines

On 1 February 1929 the United Aircraft and Transport Corporation was formed by Pratt & Whitney (the aero engine manufacturer) and the Boeing Aircraft Company. On 30 June of the same year Stout Air Services and Ford were purchased, followed on 7 May 1930 by National Air Transport. Varney Airlines became a subsidiary on 30 June 1931. Thus on 1 July 1931 all the carriers came together under the name of United Airlines Inc which was formed as a holding company for the member airlines. Pennsylvania Central Airlines merged with United in 1936, and with it came some of the former

United Air Lines (continued)

airline's Boeing 247Ds, joined in January 1940 by the Douglas DC-3. After World War II United began services to Hawaii with Douglas DC-4s. The airline's first jet was delivered on 29 May 1959, a Douglas DC-8-11, entering service on 18 September and being followed by the Boeing 720-22 in July 1960. On 1 June 1961 United took over Capital Airlines, and as a result of this acquisition United operated to 116 cities with a fleet of 267 aircraft. The most numerous single type that the airline currently operates is the Boeing 727, the first example of which was delivered on 29 October 1963 and began services on 6 February 1964 between San Francisco and Denver. On 23 July 1970 United Airlines began services with the Boeing 747 on

flights to Hawaii. Two other wide-body airliners are operated by the airline, namely the Boeing 767 and Douglas DC-10, together with Boeing 727s and 737s plus DC-8s on services to over 100 cities in the USA, plus international services to Canada, Mexico and Hawaii. Additionally, charter work is undertaken by the Western world's largest airline.

Fleet:
Boeing 727
Boeing 737
Boeing 747
Boeing 767
Douglas DC-8
Douglas DC-10

US Air

The present-day US Air was formed on 5 March 1937 as All American Aviation to operate mail services. Passenger services with Douglas DC-3s began on 7 March 1949. On 1 January 1953 All American became known as Allegheny Airlines. The first turboprop airliner operated by the airline, although only briefly, was the Convair CV-540 (a Convair CV-340 with British-built Napier engines) which it flew in 1962. In common with other US local operators the airline bought jet-powered aircraft: the first, a Douglas DC-9-14, was leased on 29 July 1966. A year later airline operating regulations were lifted and Allegheny began flying throughout the north east of the USA. Also in 1967 Allegheny formed Allegheny Commuter Lines, which brought together many

small operators to fly local services that connected with the parent airline. On 14 March 1968 Lake Central Airlines was purchased, followed by Mohawk Airlines on 14 December 1971. Thus Allegheny finally ceased to be a local service carrier and on 28 October 1979 officially adopted its current title of US Air. During the 1970s Boeing 727s and more DC-9s were purchased, and with the Boeing 737-2B7 (first delivered on

US Air is another of the massive nationwide domestic carriers in the United States, operating the Boeing 727 in large numbers alongside the 737 and DC-9.

102

The West's largest airline, United operates vast numbers of Boeing 727s throughout America.

US Air (continued)

18 November 1982) Boeing 737-4B7 (first delivered on 28 November 1984) and BAC One-Eleven, US Air operates a network of routes to 100 cities in 27 states of the USA, plus flights to Canada.

Fleet:
BAC One-Eleven
Boeing 727
Boeing 737
Douglas DC-9

UTA

Union de Transport Aériens was formed on 1 October 1963 by the merger of two French independent airlines, namely Cie de Transports Aériens Intercontinentaux (TAI, founded on 1 June 1946) and Union Aéromaritime de Transport (UAT, formed in November 1949). Throughout their histories both airlines had operated flights to French colonies in Asia, Africa and the Pacific islands. Currently UTA flies to more than 30 points in Africa and to destinations in the Middle East, Asia and the Pacific islands, as well as Los Angeles. Charters and inclusive tours are also undertaken. Most of the airline's fleet are wide-body aircraft, comprising the Douglas DC-10-30

(first delivered on 18 February 1973) and Boeing 747 (first delivered on 26 September 1978), supplemented by a small fleet of Douglas DC-8s which are shortly to be sold.

Fleet:
Boeing 747
Douglas DC-8
Douglas DC-10

VARIG

Empresa de Viaçao Aérea Rio Grandense (VARIG) was formed on 7 May 1927 and began operations on 15 June with a Dornier Wal flying-boat. International services began on 5 August 1942. On 2 August 1955 Lockheed L-1049G Super Constellations began flights from Rio de Janeiro to New York, and on 19 December 1959 VARIG began jet services to New York with the Sud-Aviation Caravelle. This French twin-jet was soon replaced by the Boeing 707, of

which the first was delivered in June 1960. In August 1961 VARIG took over REAL (Redes Estaduais Aéreas Ltda) and became the largest operator in South America; four

VARIG operates the Douglas DC-10 mainly on flights to the United States and Europe.

VARIG (continued)

years later, in February 1965, Panair do Brasil was also absorbed. On the domestic scene the turboprop-powered Hawker Siddeley 748 began to replace Douglas DC-3s and Convair CV-240s in November 1967. During the late 1960s further Boeing 707s were delivered, allowing services to Tokyo and Johannesburg to be started. On 29 May 1971 the airline's first wide-body airliner was delivered, namely the Douglas DC-10-30. In June 1975 Cruzeiro do Sul was acquired: although owned by VARIG this retains its own identity. In 1981 two further wide-body types were bought, namely the

Airbus A300 and Boeing 747. At present VARIG operates an extensive network of domestic and regional services, and has an international system that includes the Americas, Europe, Asia and Africa.

Fleet:
Airbus A300
Boeing 707
Boeing 727
Boeing 737
Boeing 747
Douglas DC-10
Lockheed L-188 Electra

VASP

Formed by the state government of Sao Paulo on 4 November 1933, VASP (Viaçao Aérea Sáo Paulo SA) began scheduled operations on 16 September 1934 from Sao Paulo. In 1947 the Douglas DC-3 entered service on an expanded network, and in July 1950 six Saab Scandias entered service; eventually 18 of this rare type were used. On 28 October 1958 the airline's first turboprop airliner was delivered, a Vickers Viscount 827. VASP began jet services with two BAC One-Eleven 422s on 19 December 1967. The carrier currently operates two Boeing types (Boeing 727 and 737) and the Airbus A300 (first delivered 5 Novem-

ber 1982) on services within Brazil, stretching from Manaus in the north to Port Alegre in the south.

Fleet:
Airbus A300
Boeing 727
Boeing 737

VIASA

Venezolana Internacional de Aviacion SA (VIASA) was formed when the Venezuelan government encouraged AVENSA (Aero-

vias Venezolanas SA) and LAV (Linea Aeropostal Venezolana) to unite in January 1961; the resulting airline was intended

VIASA has an all-Douglas fleet, with the DC-10 at the top of the tree, flying long-haul services. The DC-9 operates the shorter hauls.

VIASA (continued)

specifically to operate international services from a base at Caracas. Technical and marketing aid was and is still given by the Dutch airline KLM. Early operations were carried out by leased Douglas DC-8s, with which services to the USA, UK, France and the Netherlands were launched in mid-1961. On 24 April 1975 the first leased KLM Douglas DC-10-30 was delivered, and this type is currently the mainstay of the airline's long-haul fleet, supplemented by Douglas DC-8s. The short-haul network is operated by Douglas DC-9s. At present

scheduled passenger and cargo flights are flown to the USA, South America, Latin America and Europe.

Fleet:
Douglas DC-8
Douglas DC-9
Douglas DC-10

Wardair

Polaris Charter Co. Ltd was formed in 1946 by Maxwell Ward with a single de Havilland Fox Moth to operate charter services from a base at Yellowknife; in 1952 the airline adopted the name of Wardair Limited. It continued operating local charters for the next 10 years, but in 1962 the airline entered the transatlantic charter business with Douglas DC-6Bs and changed its name to Wardair Canada. The DC-6B was succeeded by the Boeing 727-11, of which the first was delivered on 25 April 1966. The airline's first wide-body airliner was the Boeing 747-1D1 (delivered on 23 April

1973) and with the Douglas DC-10-30 the two types operate Wardair's worldwide charter service.

Fleet:
Boeing 747
Douglas DC-10

Western Air Lines

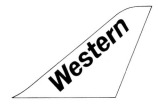

On 13 July 1925 Harris M. 'Pop' Hanshue formed Western Air Express to operate mail and passenger services. But five years later, on 16 July 1930, the airline merged with Transcontinental Air Transport to form Transcontinental and Western Airlines (TWA). It was fully absorbed into the new airline on 17 April 1934, only to reappear as a separate entity on 29 December 1934. The present name was adopted on 11 April 1941: at that time the airline had a fleet of seven Douglas DC-3s and five Boeing 247Ds. After World War II Western acquired Douglas DC-4s and Convair CV-240s for its domestic schedule. On 15 July 1957 with Douglas DC-6Bs, the first international route from Los Angeles to Mexico City was started. The first and only turboprop aircraft operated by the carrier was the Lockheed L-188 Electra, which entered service on 1 August 1959. Just under two years later, on 20 May 1961, the airline's first pure jet, a

Boeing 720-047B, was delivered to replace a leased Boeing 707. In September 1971 Western Air Lines ordered the Douglas DC-10-10, of which the first was delivered on 23 April 1973. With this and a large fleet of Boeing 727s and 737s, the airline operates scheduled passenger and cargo services to over 60 destinations in the USA, plus international services to Mexico and Canada.

Fleet:
Boeing 727
Boeing 737
Douglas DC-10

Western Air Lines (continued)

Western Air Lines operates almost exclusively in the North American continent. Long-haul and high-density sectors are flown by the Douglas DC-10.

World Airways

Incorporated on 29 March 1948, World Airways began operations with Boeing 314 flying-boats, which were replaced in 1949 by two Curtiss C-46s for charter flights from the airline's base at Oakland, California. During the late 1950s and early 1960s World was awarded its first military charters, and to cope with the extra work Douglas DC-4s/DC-6s, and Lockheed L-1049H Super Constellations were bought. On 1 April 1963 the airline was awarded an overseas charter licence and on 16 July of the same year the first jet was delivered, a Boeing 707-370. To help further expansion in the charter business, Douglas DC-8-63s were purchased in March 1971, and additional enlargement of passenger capacity was achieved in 1973 when the first Boeing 747-273C entered service between Los Angeles and London on 12 May. World's first Douglas DC-10-30CF was delivered on 7 March 1978. Currently World operates only DC-10s on long-haul scheduled services within the USA and to Honolulu, London and Frankfurt, but the main work of the airline is still worldwide charters and its contracts for the US Military Airlift Command.

Fleet:
Boeing 747
Douglas DC-10

World Airways at present only operates the Douglas DC-10, often on military charters for the US government.

Yemenia

Yemen Airlines began operations in 1951 with Douglas DC-3s on domestic and regional services. In 1962 the airline was nationalized. During the 1970s Boeing 727s and 737s were leased, this enabling the airline to expand its network. The present name, Yemenia, was adopted on 1 July 1978 when the airline was reorganized by the Yemen government (51 per cent) and Saudi Arabian government (49 per cent). Yemenia currently operates flights through-

out the Middle East and to Athens, Rome, London, Amsterdam, Frankfurt and Larnaca with Boeing 727s and 737s, and de Havilland Canada DHC-7s.

Fleet:
Boeing 727
Boeing 737
de Havilland Canada DHC-7

Zambia Airways

Formed as a subsidiary of Central African Airways in April 1964, Zambia Airways began operations on 1 July 1964 with two Douglas DC-3s and de Havilland Canada Beavers. In September 1967 the airline became totally owned by the Zambian government following the collapse of CAA. In January 1968 domestic and regional jet services were started with BAC One-Elevens, later replaced by Hawker Siddeley 748s and a Boeing 737. In November 1968 services to London from Lusaka started with leased Alitalia Douglas DC-8s, subsequently replaced by Boeing 707s in 1974. On 31 July 1984 Zambia Airways took delivery of its first wide-body airliner, a new Douglas DC-10-30 which has replaced the Boeing 707 on the London route. Scheduled passenger and cargo services are operated domestically and to neigh-

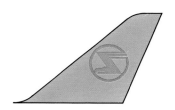

bouring countries with the Boeing 737 and HS 748, and on its long-distance flights within Africa and to Mauritius, London, Rome, Larnaca, Bombay and Sri Lanka the airline uses its Douglas DC-10 and Boeing 707s.

Fleet:
Boeing 707
Boeing 737
Douglas DC-10
Hawker Siddeley HS.748

Domestic services throughout Zambia are flown by the British Aerospace (HS) 748. The good rough-field characteristics of the type are useful in this environment.

108

Major Commercial Aircraft of the World

Aérospatiale Caravelle

Aérospatiale Caravelle 12 of Sterling Airways.

History and Notes
The Sud-Est (subsequently Aérospatiale) SE 210 Caravelle was the first turbojet-powered airliner of French design and construction. It introduced a then-unique powerplant installation with two engines in pods, one on each side of the rear fuselage, to ensure improved wing performance and a quieter cabin.

The SE 210-01 prototype (F-WHHH), powered by 10,000-lb (4536-kg) thrust Rolls-Royce Avon RA.26 turbojets, made its maiden flight on 27 May 1955, and Caravelle Is first entered service with SAS on 26 April 1959. Subsequent variants have included the generally-similar Caravelle Ia, Caravelle III with more powerful engines, Caravelle VI-N without and Caravelle VI-R with thrust-reversers, the Caravelle 10R with turbofan engines, a slightly-lengthened mixed passenger/cargo Caravelle 11B, a further 'stretched' Caravelle Super B, and the ultimate Caravelle 12 with a fuselage of still greater length, and performance improvements resulting from more powerful Pratt & Whitney JT8D engines. Production of all versions (including prototypes) totalled 280, major operators being Air France, Air Inter, Alitalia, Iberia, SAS, Sterling Airways and United Airlines. Just under 100 of these aircraft now remain in service.

Two variants were produced from Caravelle III airframes, a Caravelle VII prototype with General Electric CJ805-23C turbofans, and one given 12,200-lb (5534-kg) thrust Avon engines to serve as prototype of the Caravelle VI.

Specification: Aérospatiale Caravelle 12
Origin: France
Type: short/medium-range transport
Accommodation: flight crew of 3; up to 140 passengers
Powerplant: two 14,500-lb (6577-kg) thrust Pratt & Whitney JT8D-9 turbofans
Performance: maximum cruising speed at weight of 110,231 lb (50000 kg) 513 mph (826 km/h) at 25,000 ft (7620 m); range with maximum payload of 29,101 lb (13200kg) and no fuel reserves 2,153 miles (3465 km)
Weights: empty 65,036 lb (29500 kg); maximum take-off 127,868 lb (58000kg)
Dimensions: span 112 ft 6 in (34.29 m); length 118 ft 10½ in (36.23 m); height 29 ft 7 in (9.02 m); wing area 1,579.12 sq ft (146.70 m²)

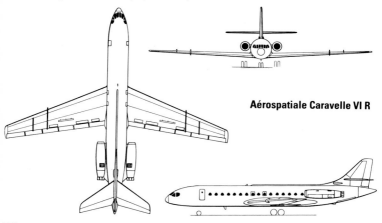

Aérospatiale Caravelle VI R

Aérospatiale/BAe Concorde

Aérospatiale/British Aerospace Concorde of Air France.

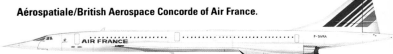

History and Notes

Numbered among the most famous civil airliners of aviation history, Concorde has the distinction of being the world's first supersonic transport (SST) to inaugurate scheduled passenger operations. These began on 21 January 1976 when Air France and British Airways began Paris-Rio de Janeiro and London-Bahrain services respectively. In 1985 the Concorde remains the only SST operating scheduled services, the Soviet Union's Tupolev Tu-144 having been withdrawn after a comparatively short operational life.

Development of SSTs was seen to be possible after flights by early supersonic bombers, and their potential time-saving for long-range flights suggested a big demand. After successful early testing, followed by demonstration and sales tours, this appeared to be confirmed by an order book totalling more than 70 aircraft from 12 major airlines. But by the time that services were inaugurated in 1976, escalating costs and anti-Concorde environmentalists had reduced the order book to nine Concordes for Air France and British Airways. Since then seven more production Concordes have been built, each manufacturer retaining one for development purposes and the two founder airlines each operating seven. Despite such limited production, Concorde has proved a supreme technological success.

Specification: Aérospatiale/British Aerospace Concorde
Origin: France/UK
Type: supersonic commercial transport
Accommodation: flight crew of 3; single-class layout for 100 passengers
Powerplant: four Rolls-Royce/SNECMA Olympus 593 Mk 610 turbojets, each developing 38,050-lb (17259-kg) thrust with afterburning
Performance: cruising speed for optimum range Mach 2.04 at 51,300 ft (15635 m), equivalent to 1,354 mph (2179 km/h); service ceiling 60,000 ft (18290 m); range with maximum payload and reserves 3,870 miles (6228 km)
Weights: empty operating 173,500 lb (78698 kg); maximum take-off 408,000 lb (185066 kg)
Dimensions: span 83 ft 10 in (25.55 m); length 203 ft 9 in (62.10 m); height 37 ft 5 in (11.40 m); wing area 3,856.0 sq ft (358.22 m²)

Aérospatiale/British Aerospace Concorde

Airbus A300

Airbus A300B2-203 of Japan's Toa Domestic Airlines.

History and Notes

At the time that Boeing in the USA was finalizing its Model 747 wide-body transport, studies were initiated in the UK for a short-range civil airliner to carry 200 passengers, a size that BEA considered ideal for future requirements. In late 1965 eight European airlines met to consider proposals, but emphasized that a larger-capacity aircraft was needed in Europe's crowded airspace. Continuing discussions led to an alignment of Hawker Siddeley, Sud-Aviation (later Aérospatiale) and West Germany represented by Arbeitgemeinschaft Airbus (later Deutsche Airbus GmbH) as the design/production team. Fokker (Netherlands) and Construcciones Aeronauticas SA (Spain) joined later the company established in December 1970 as Airbus Industrie.

First to fly was the A300B1, on 28 October 1972, with the first A300B2, representing the basic production version, on 28 June 1973. The A300B2 entered service with Air France on 30 May 1974; it was soon found to be quiet in operation, economical, reliable, and easy to maintain and operate. What had once seemed a gamble became a major success story, with orders and options for A300s from 40 airlines in 29 countries totalling more than 300. Major operators include Air France (19), Eastern Air Lines (34), Indian Airlines (10), Saudia (11) and Thai International (10).

Specification: Airbus Industrie A300B4-200

Origin: International
Type: wide-body short/medium-range transport
Accommodation: flight crew of 3; up to 336 passengers
Powerplant: two 52,500-lb (23814-kg) thrust General Electric CF6-50C1 turbofans
Performance: maximum cruising speed 566 mph (911 km/h) at 25,000 ft (7620 m); long-range cruising speed 526 mph (847 km/h) at 31,000 ft (9450 m); range with 269 passengers, baggage and fuel reserves 3,340 miles (5375 km)
Weights: basic empty 176,000 lb (79832 kg); maximum take-off 363,763 lb (165000 kg)
Dimensions: span 147 ft 1¼ in (44.84 m); length 175 ft 11 in (53.62 m); height 54 ft 2¾ in (16.53 m); wing area 2,798.71 sq ft (260.00 m²)

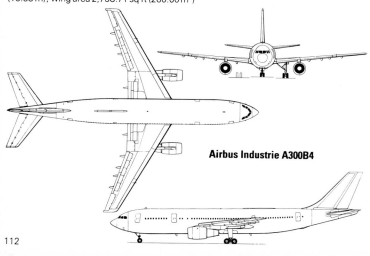

Airbus Industrie A300B4

Airbus A310

Airbus A310 of Swissair.

History and Notes

To meet European and world airline requirements for a large-capacity short-range airliner, Airbus Industrie finalized the design and layout of the A310, which shares much component commonality with the A300. A decision to proceed with its development was made in July 1978 and the first of three prototypes (F-WZLH) made its maiden flight on 3 April 1982. Certification was gained in early 1983 with entry into service, initially with Lufthansa and Swissair, following shortly afterwards.

The A310 differs from the A300 by having a fuselage of reduced length to provide standard accommodation for 210 to 255 passengers with a maximum of 282 in high-density seating, a new advanced-technology wing of slightly reduced span, new and smaller horizontal tail surfaces, modified landing gear and new underwing pylons able to mount any of the alternative powerplants that are available from General Electric, Pratt & Whitney or Rolls-Royce. The initial production version has the designation A310-200, but an A310C-200 convertible, A310F-200 freighter and a long-range development known as the A310-300 are planned.

Orders and options for the A310 total 192 for service with 17 airlines, major firm orders received from Lufthansa (25), KLM (10), Kuwait AW (10) and Swissair (10).

Specification: Airbus Industrie A310-200
Origin: International
Type: wide-body short/medium-range transport
Accommodation: flight crew of 2; up to 282 passengers
Powerplant: two 48,000-lb (21772-kg) thrust Pratt & Whitney JT9D-7R4D1 turbofans
Performance: maximum cruising speed 556 mph (895 km/h) at 30,000 ft (9145 m); long-range cruising speed 515 mph (828 km/h) at 37,000 ft (11280 m); range with 218 passengers and fuel reserves 3,224 miles (6448 km)
Weights: empty operating 169,525 lb (76895 kg); maximum take-off 313,055 lb (142000 kg)
Dimensions: span 144 ft 0¼ in (43.90 m); length 153 ft 1½ in (46.67 m); height 51 ft 10½ in (15.81 m); wing area 2,357.37 sq ft (219.00 m²)

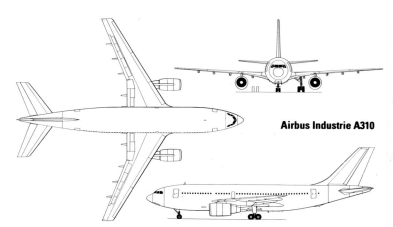

Airbus Industrie A310

Antonov An-24

Antonov An-24RV of Romania's national airline, Tarom.

History and Notes

In late 1957 the Antonov bureau designed a 32/40-seat short/medium-range transport which it designated An-24, and the first of two prototypes was flown during April 1960. A cantilever high-wing monoplane, the An-24 has a wing incorporating high-lift devices to facilitate operations from a wide variety of airfields. Tricycle landing gear has twin wheels on each unit, with provision for varying tyre pressures in flight, and power is provided by two Ivchenko AI-24A turboprops.

Early production aircraft were delivered to Aeroflot in 1962, but it was September 1963 before the first 50-seat An-24Vs were used in revenue service. Subsequent versions include the An-24V Srs II with a variety of interiors; a similar An-24RV with an auxiliary turbojet to serve as an APU at remote airfields, or to improve performance; a specialized freighter with ventral freight door, designated An-24T or An-24RT with an auxiliary turbojet installed. An An-24P equipped to drop parachute-equipped firefighters was evaluated. Production of An-24s totalled about 1,000.

Closely related versions include the An-26 freighter with more powerful engines and large rear ramp/door; the An-30, basically a survey version of the An-26; and the An-32, a specialized 'hot-and-high' short/medium-range transport. This has 5,180-ehp. (3863-kW) Ivchenko AI-20M turboprops for improved performance. Users include Balkan/Bulgarian Airlines, CAAC, Cubana, LOT and Tarom.

Specification: Antonov An-24V

Origin: USSR
Type: short-range transport
Accommodation: flight crew of 5; up to 50 passengers
Powerplant: two 2,550-ehp (1902-ekW) Ivchenko AI-24A turboprops
Performance: cruising speed 280 mph (450 km/h); service ceiling 27,560 ft (8400 m); range with maximum payload 342 miles (550 km)
Weights: empty 29,321 lb (13300 kg); maximum take-off 49,295 lb (22360 kg)
Dimensions: span 95 ft 9½ in (29.20 m); length 77 ft 2½ in (23.53 m); height 27 ft 3½ in (8.32 m); wing area 807.1 sq ft (74.98 m²)

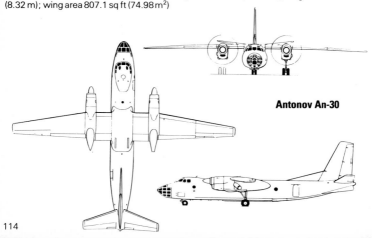

Antonov An-30

The Antonov An-26 features a rear loading ramp door and fewer windows than the An-24, and is mainly used for light transport duties. This example is seen at Havana airport.

Boeing Model 707

Boeing 707-320 of Sudan Airways.

History and Notes

Flown first on 15 July 1954, Boeing's Model 367-80 prototype was used initially as a military demonstrator. With a Boeing-designed inflight-refuelling boom it was able to show the USAF the potential of a turbojet-powered inflight-refuelling tanker. Boeing won an initial contract for 29 KC-135A tanker/transports and eventually built more than 800 aircraft under basic C-135 and C-137 designations.

The 'Dash-80' was then equipped as a civil demonstrator, gaining an order from Pan American for six Model 707-120s on 13 October 1955. The airline operated its first service on 26 October 1958, and when production ended in late 1980 967 had been delivered. They included the Model 707-020 (original designation of the Model 720), the Model 707-120, Model 707-120B (with turbofans) and Model 707-220 domestic models; and the Model 707-320, Model 707-320B (turbofans), Model 707-320C cargo or mixed cargo/passenger, and Model 707-420 (Rolls-Royce Conway powered) long-range versions. Final production version was the Model 707-320C Convertible, multi-purpose aircraft carrying up to 219 passengers. Powerplants varied from the 9,500-lb (4309-kg) thrust Pratt & Whitney JT3P turbojets of the prototype to the 19,000-lb (8618-kg) thrust turbofans of the final version. The superb Model 707 served with most of the world's major airlines and almost 300 remain in use.

Specification: Boeing 707-320C Convertible

Origin: USA
Type: commercial transport
Accommodation: flight crew of 3 or 4; up to 219 passengers
Powerplant: four 19,000-lb (8618-kg) thrust Pratt & Whitney JT3D-7 turbofans
Performance: maximum cruising speed 605 mph (974 km/h); economic cruising speed 550 mph (885 km/h); service ceiling 39,000 ft (11885 m); range with maximum fuel, reserves and 147 passengers 5,755 miles (9262 km)
Weights: empty operating, passenger 146,400 lb (66406 kg); maximum take-off 333,600 lb (151318 kg)
Dimensions: span 145 ft 9 in (44.42 m); length 152 ft 11 in (46.61 m); height 42 ft 5 in (12.93 m); wing area 3,050.0 sq ft (283.35 m²)

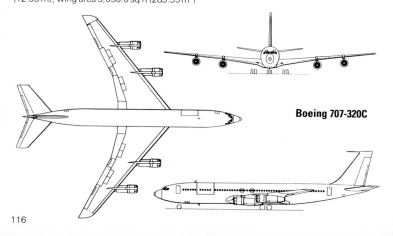

Boeing 707-320C

Boeing Model 720

Boeing 720B of Monarch Airlines.

History and Notes

The early success of the Boeing 707 led to development of an intermediate range version designated initially Model 707-020. Similar externally to the Model 707-120, the Model 707-020 introduced aerodynamic refinements and, because there were also powerplant and structural changes, the designation Model 720 was allocated.

The major aerodynamic refinements were to the wing leading edge, which also gained four additional segments of flaps, making it the first of the family to have full-span leading-edge flaps. Fuselage length was reduced by 7 ft 9 in (2.36 m) in comparison with that of the Models 707-120/-220 which, together with a reduced fuel load made it possible to lighten the structure. Typical accommodation was for 38 first and 74 tourist-class passengers. The basic model, powered by four 12,500-lb (5670-kg) thrust Pratt & Whitney JT3C-7 turbojets, flew for the first time on 23 November 1959 and entered service, initially with United Airlines, on 5 July 1960. It was followed by the improved Model 720B, flown on 6 October 1960 and first used by American Airlines on 12 March 1961.

However, there was only limited demand for the smaller-capacity Model 720/720Bs, and production ended during 1969 after a total of 154 had been delivered. About a quarter of this number now remain in service, the major operator being Middle East Airlines.

Specification: Boeing Model 720B
Origin: USA
Type: intermediate-range commercial transport
Accommodation: flight crew of 4; up to 165 passengers
Powerplant: four 18,000-lb (8165-kg) thrust Pratt & Whitney JT3D-3 turbofans
Performance: maximum cruising speed 611 mph (983 km/h) at 25,000 ft (7620 m); economic cruising speed 557 mph (896 km/h) at 40,000 ft (12190 m); service ceiling 42,000 ft (12800 m); range with maximum payload and no reserves 4,155 miles (6687 km)
Weights: empty operating 112,883 lb (51203 kg); maximum take-off 234,000 lb (106141 kg)
Dimensions: span 130 ft 10 in (39.88 m); length 136 ft 9 in (41.68 m); height 41 ft 6½ in (12.66 m); wing area 2,521.0 sq ft (234.20 m²)

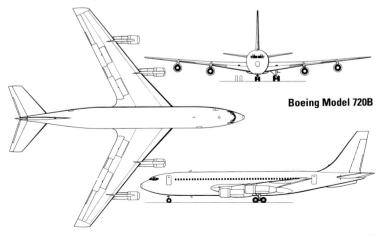

Boeing Model 720B

Boeing Model 727

Boeing 727-113C of Ariana Afghan Airlines.

History and Notes

Numbered among the world's classic airliners, Boeing's short/medium-range Model 727 was first announced on 5 December 1960. A new advanced wing was developed to cater for low-speed/short-field operations and to provide economic low-altitude/high-speed cruising capability; it brought also selection of a rear-mounted engine installation to ease wing development. The upper lobe of the Model 707 fuselage was adopted, but a new reduced-height lower fuselage was used as less cargo/baggage space was needed. The design incorporated two important features: a ventral airstair and an auxiliary power unit, allowing independent operation at small airports.

The first Model 727-100 was flown on 9 February 1963, Eastern Air Lines first using Model 727s in service on 1 February 1964. This basic version was followed by a convertible cargo/passenger Model 727-100C and a quick-change cargo or passenger Model 727-100QC, both available in 1966. A similar Model 727-200, differing by having a fuselage lengthened by 10 ft (3.05 m), entered service in 1967. From it was developed the current higher gross weight Advanced 727-200 and all-cargo Advanced 727-200F, introduced in 1973 and 1981 (respectively). When production ended in 1984 a total of 1,832 Model 727s of all versions had been ordered, of which almost 1,700 served with some 100 airlines. Major operators, each with over 100 aircraft, are American Airlines, Delta Air Lines, Eastern Air Lines and United Airlines.

Specification: Boeing Advanced 727-200
Origin: USA
Type: commercial airliner
Accommodation: flight crew of 3; up to 189 passengers
Powerplant: three 14,500-lb (6577-kg) thrust Pratt & Whitney JT8D-9A turbofans
Performance: maximum cruising speed 599 mph (964 km/h) at 24,700 ft (7530 m); economic cruising speed 542 mph (872 km) at 30,000 ft (9145 m); typical range with fuel reserves 2,303 miles (3,706 km)
Weights: empty operating 100,000 lb (45,359 kg); maximum take-off 209,500 lb (95028 kg)
Dimensions: span 108 ft 0 in (32.92 m); length 153 ft 2 in (46.69 m); height 34 ft 0 in (10.36 m); wing area 1,700.0 sq ft (157.93 m²)

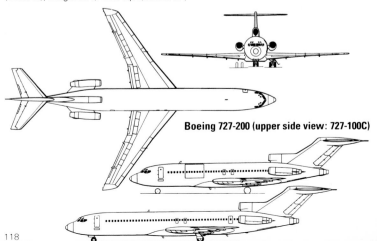

Boeing 727-200 (upper side view: 727-100C)

The Boeing Model 727 is one of the world's most widely used airliners, being employed in vast fleets by the large American carriers. European operators such as Iberia use the 727 for medium-haul routes around the sub-continent.

Boeing Model 737

Boeing 737-298C Advanced of Air Zaïre.

History and Notes

Boeing announced in 1965 the Model 737 short-range transport. It incorporated a wing similar to the Model 727, a fuselage basically that of the Model 727 but without the airstair and sized for a maximum 115 passengers, and a tail similar to that of the Model 707. A first Model 737-100 flew on 9 April 1967, Lufthansa using the type first on 10 February 1968. It was followed by a developed Model 737-200 with a lengthened fuselage for up to 130 passengers. United Airlines introduced this version on 29 April 1968; a year later Model 737-200C convertible and Model 737-200QC quick-change models became available. New versions announced in 1971 included the Advanced 737-200, available also in -200C and -200QC variants, all equipped to operate from airfields as short as 4,000 ft (1220 m); they remain in production in 1985. Business/executive versions have included the Model 737-200 Business Jet, Advanced 737-200 Business Jet and current Advanced 737-200 Executive Jet. Higher gross weight versions are available for longer-range use.

In 1980 work began to develop a larger-capacity Model 737-300. It incorporates refinements to the wing, a lengthened fuselage for a maximum 149 passengers, and new-generation fuel-efficient turbofan engines. Its first flight was made on 24 February 1984. Orders for all versions comfortably exceed 1,200 and more than 900 are in service with some 100 airlines. The total includes 19 Model 737-200s modified as T-43A navigation trainers for the USAF.

Specification: Boeing Advanced 737-200
Origin: USA
Type: commercial transport
Accommodation: flight crew of 2; up to 130 passengers
Powerplant: two 16,000-lb (7257-kg) thrust Pratt & Whitney JT8D-17A turbofans
Performance: maximum cruising speed 532 mph (856 km/h) at 33,000 ft (10060 m); range with 115 passengers and reserve fuel 2,136 miles (3438 km)
Weights: empty operating 61,630 lb (27955 kg); maximum take-off 128,100 lb (58105 kg)
Dimensions: span 93 ft 0 in (28.35 m); length 100 ft 2 in (30.53 m); height 37 ft 0 in (11.28 m); wing area 980.0 sq ft (91.04 m²)

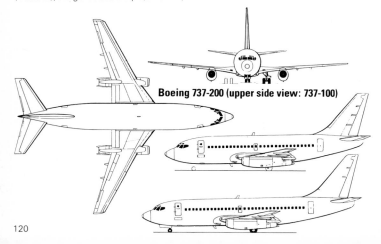

Boeing 737-200 (upper side view: 737-100)

Boeing Model 747

Boeing 747-124 of Avianca.

History and Notes

Boeing announced simultaneously on 13 April 1966 that it was to begin manufacture of a new wide-body long-range transport, and that Pan American had concluded a $525 million contract for 25 of these aircraft and spares. Its dimensions and capacity fired the imagination of journalists who soon dubbed it 'jumbo jet', a name to become better known than the official Model 747. No prototype was built and the first production aircraft was flown on 9 February 1969; Pan American inaugurated its first New York-London service with the type on 22 January 1970.

The Model 747 has a wing incorporating features developed for other members of the family, tricycle landing gear that has four four-wheel main bogies, and a cabin 187 ft (57 m) long and 20 ft 1½ in (6.13 m) wide: in the initial Model 747-100 this provided accommodation for a maximum of 490 passengers. Currently available versions include the Model 747-100B with strengthened structure; the similar-capacity Model 747-200B operating at higher weights; the Model 747SR short-range version of the Model 747-100B; the Model 747-200B Combi for all-passenger or passenger/cargo operations; the Model 747-200C Convertible for all-passenger, all-cargo or combinations of both; and the all-cargo Model 747-200F Freighter.

Orders for all versions of the Model 747 are well past the 600 mark; major operators include Air France, British Airways, Japan Airlines, Northwest Airlines and Pan American.

Specification: Boeing 747-200B

Origin: USA
Type: heavy commercial transport
Accommodation: flight crew of 3; up to 516 passengers, this including 32 on upper deck
Powerplant: four 54,750-lb (24834-kg) thrust Pratt & Whitney JT9D-7R4G2 turbofans
Performance: maximum speed 602 mph (969 km/h) at 30,000 ft (9145 m); cruise ceiling 45,000 ft (13715 m); range with fuel reserves and 452 passengers 6,563 miles (10,562 km)
Weights: empty operating 382,000 lb (173272 kg); maximum take-off 833,000 lb (377842 kg)
Dimensions: span 195 ft 8 in (59.64 m); length 231 ft 10 in (70.66 m); height 63 ft 5 in (19.33 m); wing area 5,500.0 sq ft (510.95 m^2)

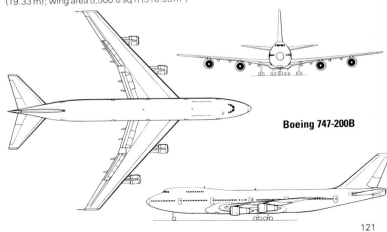

Boeing 747-200B

Boeing Model 747SP

Boeing 747SP of the Taiwanese line, China Airlines.

History and Notes

On 3 September 1973 Boeing announced that the company intended to develop a lighter-weight longer-range version of the Model 747 for use on lower-density routes. News came a week later than Pan American had ordered 10 of these aircraft, identified as the Model 747SP (Special Performance).

The Model 747SP is basically similar to the Model 747-100B, the major difference being a reduction of 47 ft 1 in (14.35 m) in overall length. This provides seats for 299 passengers on the main deck and 32 on the upper deck, with a maximum high-density seating capacity of 440. Fuel tankage is also increased. One Model 747SP with 50 passengers established during 23/24 March 1976 a world record for nonstop distance by a commercial aircraft of 10,290 miles (16,560 km), on delivery from Washington to Cape Town.

The Model 747EUD (Extended Upper Deck), in 1982 redesignated Model 747-300, has the upper forward fuselage extended aft by 23 ft 4 in (7.11 m) to increase accommodation in this area from 32 to 69 passengers. This conversion is applicable to all current production versions except the Models 747-200C, -200F and 747SP. Orders for this option are now approaching the 20 mark.

Under the designation E-4 the USAF has acquired four of a planned six Model 747-200Bs equipped as Advanced Airborne Command Post (AABNCP) aircraft, to provide a vital link between the US national command and its retaliatory forces in the event of an attack on the USA.

Specification: Boeing Model 747SP
Origin: USA
Type: long-range commercial transport
Accommodation: flight crew of 3; up to 440 passengers
Powerplant: four 50,000-lb (22680-kg) thrust Pratt & Whitney JT9D-7FW turbofans
Performance: maximum speed 609 mph (980 km/h) at 30,000 ft (9145 m); service ceiling 45,100 ft (13745 m); range with fuel reserves and 331 passengers 6,736 miles (10,841 km)
Weights: empty operating 325,000 lb (147418 kg); maximum take-off 700,000 lb (317515 kg)
Dimensions: span 195 ft 8 in (59.64 m); length 184 ft 9 in (56.31 m); height 65 ft 5 in (19.94 m); wing area 5,500.0 sq ft (510.95 m²)

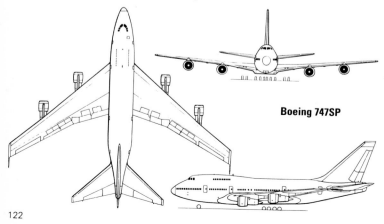

Boeing 747SP

Boeing Model 757

Boeing 757 of Eastern Airlines, one of the launch customers.

History and Notes

Boeing announced in early 1978 its intention of developing a new advanced-technology short/medium-range commercial transport. Identified as the Model 757, it has a new wing, makes use of the Model 727 fuselage and is powered by two advanced fuel-efficient turbofan engines. Following the finalization of contracts with British Airways and Eastern Air Lines for 19 and 21 aircraft respectively, Boeing announced on 23 March 1979 that production had been initiated. The first of these aircraft (N757A) was rolled out on 13 January 1982 and made its maiden flight on 19 February 1982. The initial production version is the Model 757-200, and first deliveries were made on schedule, Eastern Airlines operating its first revenue flight on 1 January 1983.

To achieve the simultaneous launch of this programme and of the Model 767, Boeing has had to rely on national and international co-operation. For example, the airframe has assemblies/components produced by Avco Aerostructures, Boeing Vertol, Fairchild Republic, Grumman, Heath Tecna and Schweizer in the US, and by CASA in Spain, Hawker de Havilland in Australia and Short Brothers in Northern Ireland. The Rolls-Royce RB.211-535 engines that powered early production aircraft have shown a fuel saving of some 53 per cent per passenger by comparison with the engines of current medium-range aircraft.

Orders for some 140 aircraft have been received, the major buyer being Delta Air Lines with 60 on order.

Specification: Boeing Model 757

Origin: USA
Type: short/medium-range commercial transport
Accommodation: flight crew of 2; up to 224 passengers
Powerplant: two 37,400-lb (16964-kg) thrust Rolls-Royce RB.211-535C turbofans
Performance: (with 186 passengers) cruising speed Mach 0.80; maximum range 2,752 miles (4429 km)
Weights: empty operating 127,050 lb (57629 kg); maximum take-off 240,000 lb (108862 kg)
Dimensions: span 124ft 10in (38.05m); length 155 ft 3 in (47.32 m); height 44 ft 6in (13.56 m); wing area 1,994.0 sq ft (185.24 m^2)

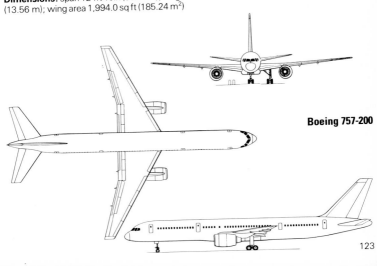

Boeing 757-200

Boeing Model 767

Boeing 767 of United Air Lines.

History and Notes

Simultaneously with the announcement of its intention to develop the Model 757, Boeing revealed that a wider-body Model 767, to permit a two-aisle seating layout, would be introduced at the same time. Definition of its design benefitted from the participation of United Air Lines, and following receipt of an order for 30 of these aircraft from UAL, Boeing announced on 14 July 1978 the initiation of full-scale development. Construction began a year later and the first (N767BA) was rolled out on 4 August 1981. This flew for the first time on 26 September, and following certification on 30 July 1982 deliveries to UAL began the following month, the airline making an inaugural flight with the type, between Chicago and Denver, on 8 September 1982.

Similar in overall configuration to the Model 757, the Model 767 differs primarily by its 15 ft 6 in (4.72 m) wide cabin and in having a flight deck specifically designed for two-crew operation. Power is provided by advanced-technology fuel-efficient engines, initially Pratt & Whitney JT9D-7R4D turbofans. As in the case of the 757, its production is the result of national/international collaboration, involving Canada, Italy and Japan as well as the USA. The initial production version is designated Model 767-200 and orders for some 190 aircraft have been received. Major operators include Air Canada, All Nippon, American Airlines, Delta Air Lines, TWA and United Airlines.

Specification: Boeing Model 767
Origin: USA
Type: medium-range commercial transport
Accommodation: flight crew of 2; up to 289 passengers
Powerplant: two 47,800-lb (21682-kg) thrust Pratt & Whitney JT9D-7R4D turbofans
Performance: cruising speed Mach 0.80; service ceiling 39,000 ft (11885 m); range 3,782 miles (6087 km)
Weights: empty operating 177,216 lb (80384 kg); maximum take-off 300,000 lb (136078 kg)
Dimensions: span 156 ft 1 in (47.57 m); length 159 ft 2 in (48.51 m); height 52 ft 0 in (15.85 m); wing area 3,050.0 sq ft (283.35 m²)

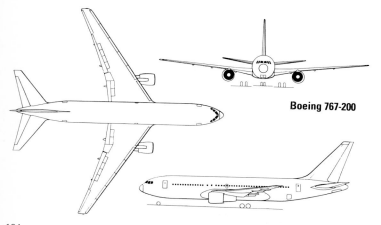

Boeing 767-200

Boeing Vertol Model 234 Chinook

Boeing Vertol 234LR Commercial Chinook of British Airways Helicopters.

History and Notes

In 1956 Boeing Vertol began the development of an all-weather transport helicopter for use by the US Army, and this entered service as the CH-47 Chinook. Its extensive use and the product improvement and refinement that results from some 20 years of military service led the company to announce in 1978 a civil counterpart for commercial use. Two versions were planned and the first to fly, on 19 August 1980, was the long-range Model 234LR which received CAA and FAA certification during June 1981. An initial order for three (increased later to six) aircraft was received from British Airways Helicopters, and this operator introduced the first into service on 1 July 1981: they are used mainly for North Sea of rig support. Other orders have been received from Arco Alaska and Helikopter Service A/S of Norway.

The Model 234LR is identified easily by fairings on each side of the fuselage, twice the size of those on military Chinooks, which house large fuel tanks. Internally the Model 234LR is equipped to airline standards for passenger, passenger/freight or all-cargo use. The utility 234UT has internal fuel tanks, the external fairings being removed. Conversion from LR to UT configuration, or vice versa, can be done in about eight hours.

Specification: Boeing Vertol Model 234LR

Origin: USA
Type: commercial transport helicopter
Accommodation: flight crew of 2; up to 44 passengers
Powerplant: two 4,075-shp (3039-kW) Avco Lycoming AL 5512 turboshafts
Performance: maximum cruising speed 167 mph (269 km/h) at 2,000 ft (610 m); economic cruising speed 155 mph (249 km/h) at 2,000 ft (610 m); operational ceiling 15,000 ft (4570 m); range with fuel reserves and 44 passengers 661 miles (1064 km)
Weights: empty operating 27,100 lb (12292 kg); maximum take-off 48,500 lb (21999 kg)
Dimensions: rotor diameter, each 60 ft 0 in (18.29 m); length, rotors turning 99 ft 0 in (30.18 m); height 18 ft 7¾ in (5.68 m); rotor disc area, total 5,654.9 sq ft (525.34 m²)

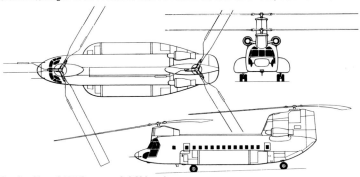

Boeing Vertol 234 Commercial Chinook

British Aerospace 146

British Aerospace 146 Series 200 of US regional carrier Air Wisconsin.

History and Notes

Hawker Siddeley began development of the HS 146 four-turbofan transport in August 1973. Within months economic problems in the UK brought virtual suspension of the programme until 10 July 1978, when it was resumed by British Aerospace. Production is being undertaken in several company factories, as well as by risk-sharing partners that include Avco Aerostructures (USA) and Saab-Scania (Sweden); Short Brothers in Northern Ireland are manufacturing pods for its Avco Lycoming engines.

Two versions are available, the HS 146 Series 100 for operation from short semi-prepared airstrips, with a seating capacity of 71-93, and a longer-fuselage (by 7 ft 10 in/2.39 m) HS 146 Series 200 for operation from paved runways with 82-109 passengers. The first Series 100 prototype (G-SSHH) was flown on 3 September 1981 and the Series 200 on 1 August 1982, with certification gained in May and June 1983 respectively. The basic configuration is of a high-wing cantilever monoplane with a pressurized circular-section fuselage, a T-tail with swept surfaces, retractable tricycle landing gear and power provided by four Avco Lycoming turbofan engines in pylon-mounted underwing pods.

Orders and options for 82 aircraft had been received by late 1984 the major customers being Air Wisconsin and Pacific Southwest Airlines.

Specification: BAe 146 Series 100
Origin: UK
Type: short-range transport
Accommodation: flight crew of 2; up to 93 passengers
Powerplant: four 6,700-lb (3039-kg) thrust Avco Lycoming ALF 502R-3 turbofans
Performance: maximum operating speed Mach 0.70; economic cruising speed 440 mph (708 km/h) at 30,000 ft (9145 m); range with fuel reserves and maximum payload 495 miles (797 km)
Weights: empty operating 47,000 lb (21319 kg); maximum take-off 82,250 lb (37308 kg)
Dimensions: span 86 ft 5 in (26.34 m); length 85 ft 10 in (26.16 m); height 28 ft 3 in (8.61m); wing area 832.0 sq ft (77.29 m²)

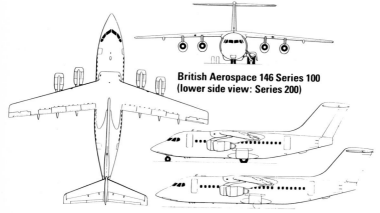

British Aerospace 146 Series 100
(lower side view: Series 200)

British Aerospace 748

British Aerospace (Avro/HS) 748 of Bahamasair.

History and Notes

Starting as an Avro project in 1958, the Type 748 was designed to provide airlines with a 20-seat feeder transport. However, it failed to gain any interest with this capacity and its design was scaled up, and then in 1959 the Hawker Siddeley Group, of which Avro was a component, decided to build four prototypes, the first (G-APZV) flying on 24 June 1960 and accommodating up to 44 passengers. Power was provided by two Rolls-Royce Dart turboprops, mounted high on the wing leading edge. The HS 748 Series 1 production version was flown first on 31 August 1961; it differed by having 1,740-eshp (1298-ekW) Dart 514 engines and seats for up to 48 passengers.

HS 748 Series 2 aircraft with 1,910-eshp (1424-ekW) Dart 531s and 52 seats were followed by HS 748 Series 2A machines with more engine power; they became available also in a Military transport version and as the HS 748 Coastguarder for maritime patrol. The Series 2A was followed by the HS 748 Series 2B introduced in 1979, marketed in the USA as the intercity 748. This had Dart 536-2 engines for improved 'hot-and-high' performance, a slight increase in wing span and other refinements and was available in the same variants as the HS 748 Series 2A. Current production version is the further improved HS 748 Series 2B Super and these introduced a number of refinements. Sales of HS 748s of all series are nearing the 400 mark in 1985, this including 31 supplied to the RAF as Andover C.Mk 1 utility transports.

Specification: BAe HS 748 Series 2B

Origin: UK
Type: passenger/freight transport
Accommodation: flight crew of 2; up to 58 passengers
Powerplant: two 2,280-eshp (1,700-ekW) Rolls-Royce Dart RDa.7 Mk 536-2 turboprops
Performance: cruising speed at weight of 38,000 lb (17237 kg) 281 mph (452 km/h); service ceiling 25,000 ft (7620 m); range with maximum payload and fuel reserves 904 miles (1455 km)
Weights: empty operating 26,910 lb (12206 kg); maximum take-off 46,500 lb (21092 kg)
Dimensions: span 102 ft 5½ in (31.23 m); length 67 ft 0 in (20.42 m); height 24 ft 10 in (7.57 m); wing area 828.87 sq ft (77.00 m²)

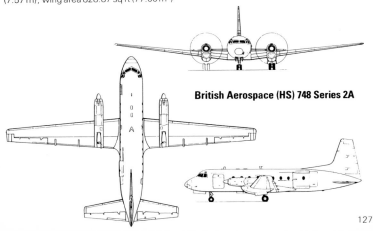

British Aerospace (HS) 748 Series 2A

British Aerospace One-Eleven

British Aerospace (BAC) One-Eleven Series 500 of Cyprus Airways.

History and Notes

The British Aerospace One-Eleven derives from the Hunting Aircraft H.107 project for a 32-seat turbojet-powered transport. In 1960 Hunting was acquired by British Aircraft Corporation, which continued development as the 59-seat BAC.107. This failed to gain interest, leading to the 79-seat BAC.111 (later named One-Eleven). The basic One-Eleven Series 200 prototype (G-ASHG) was flown first on 20 August 1963. It was introduced into service on British United Airways' Gatwick-Genoa route on 9 April 1965.

The One-Eleven Series 200 (56 built) was followed by the One-Eleven Series 300 (9) with increased payload/range capability, and the similar One-Eleven Series 400 (69) modified to US requirements. The prototype of a larger-capacity One-Eleven Series 500 was flown on 30 June 1967, its fuselage lengthened by 13 ft 6 in (4.11 m); a final variant, the One-Eleven Series 475, combined the Series 400 fuselage with Series 500 wings and powerplant: both were available in executive and freighter variants.

One-Eleven sales totalled 230, but licence construction of these aircraft continues in Romania. Two One-Eleven Srs 525/1s and one One-Eleven Srs 487 freighter were supplied to Romania as specimen aircraft during 1981-2, and Romanian production of Rombac 1-11 aircraft has been started. More than 150 of the British-built One-Elevens remain in service, major operators being British Airways, British Caledonian Airways, Dan-Air, Philippine Airlines, Tarom and US Air.

Specification: BAe One-Eleven Srs 500

Origin: UK
Type: short/medium-range transport
Accommodation: flight crew of 2; up to 119 passengers
Powerplant: two 12,550-lb (5693-kg) thrust Rolls-Royce Spey Mk 512 DW turbofans
Performance: maximum cruising speed 541 mph (871 km/h) at 21,000 ft (6400 m); maximum cruising height 35,000 ft (10670 m); range with fuel reserves and full payload 1,694 miles (2726 km)
Weights: empty operating 53,762 lb (24386 kg); maximum take-off 104,500 lb (47400 kg)
Dimensions: span 93 ft 6 in (28.50 m); length 107 ft 0 in (32.61 m); height 24 ft 6 in (7.47 m); wing area 1,031.0 sq ft (95.78 m²)

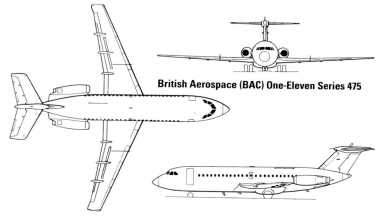

British Aerospace (BAC) One-Eleven Series 475

British Aerospace Trident

British Aerospace (DH/HS) Trident 2E of CAAC (Civil Aviation Administration of China).

History and Notes

The Trident originated as the de Havilland D.H.121, to meet a British European Airways requirement of 1956 for a short/medium-range transport. Submissions were made also by Avro and Bristol, but it was de Havilland that gained a contract for 24 D.H.121s on 12 August 1959. The first Trident I (G-ARPA) was flown on 9 January 1962. This had a 'clean' low-set monoplane wing, rear-mounted powerplant comprising three 9,850-lb (4468-kg) thrust Rolls-Royce RB.163/1 Mk 505/5 Spey turbofans, and seats for up to 103 passengers.

When de Havilland merged into the Hawker Siddeley group, the latter company became responsible for development and production of the HS 121 Trident. Later versions were the Trident 1E, with more powerful Speys and seating for a maximum 139 passengers; the further-developed Trident 2E flown on 27 July 1967 and the last major production variant, the Trident 3B. In this version the fuselage was lengthened to seat a maximum 180 passengers and a fourth engine was provided in the form of a 5,250-lb (2381-kg) thrust RB.162-86 turbojet in the aircraft's tail unit, below the rudder. The final variant comprised two Trident Super 3Bs for CAAC, national airline of the People's Republic of China. They differed from Trident 3Bs by having increased fuel and 152 seats. A total of 117 Tridents were built and about 50 remain in service, used by British Airways and CAAC.

Specification: BAe Trident 2E

Origin: UK
Type: short/medium-range transport
Accommodation: flight crew of 3; up to 139 passengers
Powerplant: three 11,960-lb (5425-kg) thrust Rolls-Royce RB.163-25 Mk 512-5W Spey turbofans
Performance: cruising speed 605 mph (974 km/h) at 25,000 ft (7620 m); economic cruising speed 596 mph (959 km/h) at 30,000 ft (9145 m); range with typical payload and fuel reserves 2,464 miles (3965 km)
Weights: empty operating 73,200 lb (33203 kg); maximum take-off 144,000 lb (65317 kg)
Dimensions: span 98 ft 0 in (29.87 m); length 114 ft 9 in (34.98 m); height 27 ft 0 in (8.23 m); wing area 1,456.0 sq ft (135.26 m²)

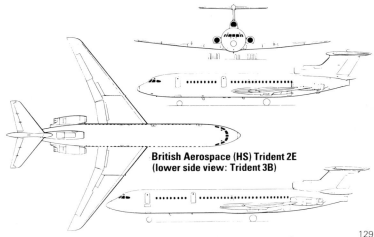

British Aerospace (HS) Trident 2E
(lower side view: Trident 3B)

de Havilland Canada DHC-6

History and Notes

De Havilland Canada announced in 1964 the development of a turboprop-powered STOL civil transport to seat 13 to 18 passengers. Designated DHC-6 Twin Otter, the first was flown on 20 May 1965. A braced high-wing monoplane with fixed tricycle landing gear, the Twin Otter has a wheeled gear installation as standard, with skis or floats optional, and power provided by two Pratt & Whitney PT6A turboprops in wing-mounted nacelles. The first three aircraft had 579-eshp (432-ekW) PT6A-6s, but Twin Otter Series 100 and Twin Otter Series 200 production aircraft have similarly-rated PT6A-20 engines.

Intended for use by commuter or third-level airlines, Twin Otters serve also with many air forces and government agencies. The first Series 100 aircraft entered service in 1966, followed by the Series 200 which has a lengthened nose and extended rear cabin to provide greater baggage capacity. The current Twin Otter Series 300 has more powerful PT6A-27 engines and a 20-seat commuter interior. Six Twin Otter Series 300S aircraft were developed for an experimental service between STOL airports in Montreal and Ottawa, and available for all versions is equipment for freight carrying and water-bombing. In mid-1982 the company announced the introduction of three Twin Otter Series 300M military versions, each with equipment for a specific role. A total of over 800 Twin Otters has been sold to operators in more than 17 countries.

de Havilland Canada DHC-6 Twin Otter of NorOntair.

Specification: de Havilland Canada DHC-6 Twin Otter Series 300 (landplane)
Origin: Canada
Type: utility STOL transport
Accommodation: flight crew of 2; up to 20 passengers
Powerplant: two 652-eshp (486-ekW) Pratt & Whitney Aircraft of Canada PT6A-27 turboprops
Performance: maximum cruising speed 210 mph (338 km/h) at 10,000 ft (3050 m); service ceiling 26,700 ft (8140 m); range with 2,500-lb (1134-kg) payload 806 miles (1297 km)
Weights: empty operating 7,415 lb (3363 kg); maximum take-off 12,500 lb (5670 kg)
Dimensions: span 65 ft 0 in (19.81 m); length 51 ft 9 in (15.77 m); height 19 ft 6 in (5.94 m); wing area 420.0 sq ft (39.02 m²)

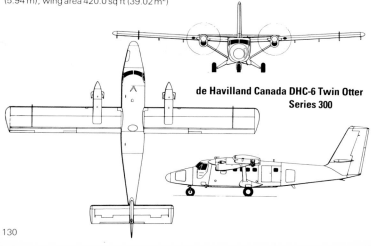

de Havilland Canada DHC-6 Twin Otter Series 300

de Havilland Canada DHC-7

de Havilland Canada DHC-7 Dash Seven of Air Pacific.

History and Notes

With backing from the Canadian government, de Havilland Canada began in late 1972 the development of a larger capacity short/medium range STOL transport that would provide the higher standards of comfort to be found in much larger airliners. Designated DHC-7, and later named Dash 7, the first of two pre-production aircraft (C-GNBX-X) made its maiden flight on 27 March 1975. The first production aircraft (C-GQIW) was flown on 30 May 1977 and about 90 are already in service, Air Wisconsin and Ransome Airlines being the major users.

In configuration the DHC-7 is a cantilever high-wing monoplane with a circular-section pressurized fuselage, T-tail, retractable tricycle landing gear with twin wheels on each unit, and power provided by four Pratt & Whitney PT6A-50 turboprops. Access to the cabin, which seats 50 passengers, is via a single airstair door at the rear of the cabin on the port side. There are provisions for optional mixed passenger/cargo or all-cargo operations, and a large freight door can be installed at the forward end of the cabin on the port side. The all-cargo version of the Dash 7 is designated Series 101, and examples serve with the Canadian Armed Forces under the designation CC-132. Orders and options for the Dash 7, received from more than 20 airlines and the Venezuelan navy, have reached a total in excess of 100.

Specification: de Havilland Canada DHC-7 Dash 7
Origin: Canada
Type: short/medium-range STOL transport
Accommodation: flight crew of 2; up to 50 passengers
Powerplant: four 1,120-shp (835-kW) Pratt & Whitney Aircraft of Canada PT6A-50 turboprops
Performance: maximum cruising speed at weight of 41,000 lb (18597 kg) 261 mph (420 km/h) at 8,000 ft (2440 m); service ceiling 21,000 ft (6400 m); range with 50 passengers and fuel reserves 795 miles (1279 km)
Weights: empty operating 27,650 lb (12542 kg); maximum take-off 44,000 lb (19958 kg)
Dimensions: span 93 ft 0 in (28.35 m); length 80 ft 7¾ in (24.58 m); height 26 ft 2 in (7.98 m); wing area 860.0 sq ft (79.89 m²)

de Havilland Canada DHC-7 Dash-7

de Havilland Canada DHC-8

de Havilland Canada DHC-8 Dash Eight of Brymon Airways.

History and Notes

To meet growing demands for a quiet short-range transport in the 30/40-seat class, de Havilland Aircraft of Canada initiated the development of such an aircraft under the designation DHC-8 and name Dash 8. It fits in between the company's 19-seat Twin Otter and 50-seat Dash 7 to make a family of aircraft covering a useful range of requirements for commuter and third-line operators. While slightly smaller, the DHC-8 has an overall configuration is similar to that of the Dash 7, being a high-wing monoplane with retractable tricycle landing gear and a T-tail. Power, however, is provided by only two engines, these being advanced-technology turboprops driving large-diameter slow-turning propellers to ensure very low noise levels. Each rated at 1,800 shp (1342 kW), the engines have automatic performance reserve so that, in the event of one engine failing, the other will automatically deliver an output of 2,000 shp (1491 kW).

The Dash 8 will be available in two versions, Commuter and Corporate. The first is the basic aircraft with accommodation for 32 passengers; the second, which will be marketed in North America exclusively by Innotech Aviation of Montreal, will have increased range capability, an auxiliary power unit as standard and will seat, typically, 16 to 24 passengers. Well over 100 orders and options for the Dash 8 have been received by de Havilland Canada, 60 per cent of them from customers in the USA, and the first aircraft made its maiden flight on 20 June 1983. The first production aircraft, for NorOntair, was delivered in October 1984.

Specification: de Havilland Canada DHC-8 Dash 8

Origin: Canada
Type: short-range transport
Accommodation: flight crew of 2; up to 36 passengers
Powerplant: two 1,800-shp (1342-kW) Pratt & Whitney Aircraft of Canada PW 120 turboprops
Performance: (estimated) maximum cruising speed 310 mph (499 km/h) at 15,000 ft (4570 m); normal range with fuel reserves 656 miles (1056 km)
Weights: empty operating 21,590 lb (9793 kg); maximum take-off 33,000 lb (14969 kg)
Dimensions: span 84 ft 11½ in (25.90 m); length 73 ft 0 in (22.25 m); height 24 ft 5 in (7.44 m); wing area 585.0 sq ft (54.35 m^2)

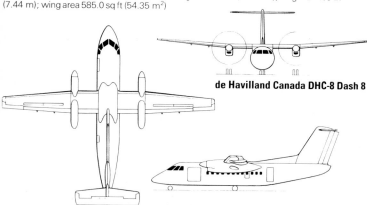

de Havilland Canada DHC-8 Dash 8

Douglas DC-8

Douglas DC-8 Series 50 of French airline UTA.

History and Notes

On 7 June 1955 Douglas Aircraft announced its intention of developing a turbojet-powered airliner to supersede the DC-7. A prototype/demonstrator DC-8 was built and when this flew, on 30 May 1958, it was seen to be similar to the Boeing 707. From the outset it was planned to make the DC-8 appeal to a wide range of operators, the type being available with seating capacities from 118 to 176 and with a variety of powerplants. Following certification, on 31 August 1959, the first services were inaugurated simultaneously by Delta Air Lines and United Airlines on 18 September 1959.

Early examples with 13,000-lb (5897-kg) thrust Pratt & Whitney JT3C-6 turbojets were designated DC-8 Series 10, the basic domestic version. The Series 20, also for domestic use, differed only by having 15,800-lb (7167-kg) thrust JT4A-3 turbojets. The Series 30, the first intended specifically for intercontinental use, retained the same airframe but had more powerful JT4A-9 engines; the Series 40, also an intercontinental version, had 17,500-lb (7398-kg) thrust Rolls-Royce Conway 509 turbofans. Finally came the Series 50 with Pratt & Whitney turbofans and with a revised interior layout to seat a maximum 189 passengers. Other specialist requirements were met by manufacture of convertible passenger/freight Series 50CFs and all-freight Series 50Fs. Production of these first DC-8s totalled 294, and about 75 Series 10 to 50 aircraft remain in service.

Specification: Douglas DC-8 Series 50

Origin: USA
Type: long-range transport
Accommodation: flight crew of 3 to 5; up to 189 passengers
Powerplant: four 18,000-lb (8165-kg) thrust Pratt & Whitney JT3D-3 turbofans
Performance: maximum cruising speed 579 mph (932 km/h) at 30,000 ft (9145 m); range with maximum payload 5,720 miles (9205 km)
Weights: empty operating 132,325 lb (60022 kg); maximum take-off 325,000 lb (147418 kg)
Dimensions: span 142 ft 5 in (43.41 m); length 150 ft 6 in (45.87 m); height 43 ft 4 in (13.21 m); wing area 2,883.0 sq ft (267.83 m²)

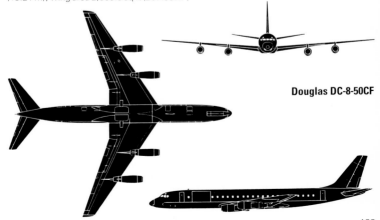

Douglas DC-8-50CF

Douglas DC-8 Super 60 and 70

Douglas DC-8 Series 70 of Overseas National Airways.

History and Notes

The basic DC-8 design showed great potential for growth and on 5 April 1965, Douglas announced a new stretched series based on the DC-8 Series 50. The first member of this new series was the Super 61, which featured a massive stretch of 36 ft 8 in (11.18 m), offering a maximum capacity of 259 passengers. Second in the series was the Super 62 which sported a new wing of increased span and a fuselage stretch of 6 ft 8 in (2.03 m). Fuel capacity was increased and this became the long-range version of the DC-8. The Super 63 combined the fuselage stretch of the Super 61 with the new wing of the Super 62 for a high-capacity, long-range airliner. All these aircraft were available in all-cargo (AF) and convertible (CF) versions.

In 1979, Douglas announced details of a plan to upgrade DC-8 Series 61, 62 and 63 aircraft by the installation of advanced-technology turbofans, the resulting conversions being designated Series 71, 72 and 73 respectively. Chosen powerplant is the General Electric/SNECMA CFM56, with the Pratt & Whitney JT8D-209 optional.

This programme is managed by Cammacorp of Los Angeles, California and in addition to engine conversion an optional auxiliary power unit and environmental control system can be installed. The first modification of a DC-8 Series 61 was completed in 1981, the resulting Super 71 making its first flight on 15 August. Since then the company has received about 130 orders and options for conversions. Douglas claim these to be the quietest large four-engined transports in service, offering a true noise reduction of some 70 per cent without any loss of performance.

Specification: Douglas DC-8 Super 72

Origin: USA
Type: extra long-range transport
Accommodation: flight crew of 3; up to 189 passengers
Powerplant: four 24,000-lb (10886-kg) thrust General Electric/SNECMA CFM56 turbofans
Performance: maximum speed 600 mph (966 km/h); cruising speed 531 mph (855 km/h) at 35,000 ft (10670 m); range with maximum payload 7,220 miles (11619 km)
Weights: empty operating 152,600 lb (69218 kg); maximum take-off 335,000 lb (151953 kg)
Dimensions: span 148 ft 5 in (45.24 m); length 157 ft 5 in (47.98 m); height 42 ft 5 in (12.93 m); wing area 2,927.0 sq ft (271.92 m²)

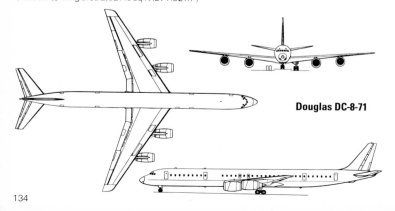

Douglas DC-8-71

Douglas DC-9

Douglas DC-9 Series 32 of the Spanish flag-carrier, Iberia.

History and Notes

The Douglas DC-9 was a completely new design with rear-mounted engines, the first prototype flying on 25 Feburary 1965. It was followed by the 80/90-seat Series 10, which was powered by Pratt & Whitney JT8D engines and entered service first with Delta Air Lines on 8 December 1965, production totalling 137. Next came the Series 30 with a fuselage lengthened by 14 ft 10¾ in (4.54 m) to seat up to 119 passengers, increased wing span and other improvements. They were used first by Eastern Air Lines on 1 February 1967.

To meet the needs of SAS Douglas developed the Series 20, combining the Series 10 fuselage and increased-span wing of the Series 30; this entered service on 23 January 1969. SAS also inspired the high-capacity short-range Series 40 which entered service in March 1968. Derived from the Series 30, it has more fuel and a fuselage lengthened to seat up to 132 passengers. Last version is the Series 50, with a 'stretch' of 14 ft 3 in (4.34 m) to seat up to 139 passengers in a modernized interior, which entered service with Swissair in August 1975. All versions were available in passenger (DC-9), cargo (DC-9F), convertible (DC-9CF) and passenger/cargo (DC-9RC) configurations. Military versions include the C-9A Nightingale and VC-9C transports of the USAF, and C-9B Skytrain II logistic transport of the US Navy. Orders for DC-9s totalled more than 1,100 before production was terminated in favour of the DC-9 Super 80 series.

Specification: Douglas DC-9 Series 50

Origin: USA
Type: short/medium-range transport
Accommodation: flight crew of 2; up to 139 passengers
Powerplant: two 15,500-lb (7031-kg) thrust Pratt & Whitney JT8D-15 turbofans
Performance: maximum speed 575 mph (925 km/h); economic cruising speed 510 mph (821 km/h); range with 97 passengers and fuel reserves 2,065 miles (3323 km)
Weights: empty 61,880 lb (28068 kg); maximum take-off 121,000 lb (54885 kg)
Dimensions: span 93 ft 5 in (28.47 m); length 133 ft 7¼ in (40.72 m); height 28 ft 0 in (8.53 m); wing area 1,000.75 sq ft (92.97 m²)

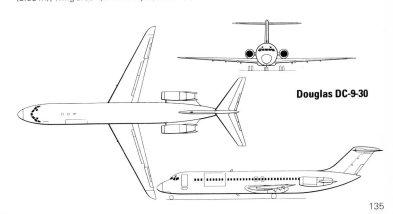

Douglas DC-9-30

Douglas DC-9 Super 80

Douglas DC-9 Series 80 of Pacific Southwest Airlines.

History and Notes

Sales of more than 1,000 examples of the Douglas DC-9 represent a major success for the company in the commercial field. This was because the DC-9 appeared on the market some two years earlier than its main rival, the Boeing 737, and also because of its availability in a range of sizes and configurations. However, the company realized that with accelerating fuel costs a worthwhile market would exist for an improved DC-9-50 of greater capacity, with quieter more fuel-efficient engines. This, in effect, describes the DC-9 Super 81 and Super 82 which were certificated on 3 September 1980 and 30 July 1981 repectively.

Developed from the basic Series 50, the Super 81 has a wing increased in span by 14 ft 5 in (4.39 m), and a fuselage lengthened by 14 ft 3 in (4.34 m) to seat up to 172 passengers in a modern 'wide-look' cabin. Gross weight is increased by some 16 per cent, made possible by advanced-technology Pratt & Whitney JT8D series 200 turbofan engines. Not only are these more powerful than the earlier JT8Ds, they are quieter and have a better specific fuel consumption. The Super 82 is generally similar, but differs by having 20,000-lb (9072-kg) thrust JT8D-217 turbofans more suited to operation from 'hot and high' airports. The first Series 81 entered service with Swissair on its Zurich-London route on 5 October 1980. The aircraft is now marketed as the McDonnell Douglas MD-80, and orders and options for the MD-81 (Super 81) and MD-82 (Super 82) and longer-range MD-83 now exceed 300.

Specification: Douglas DC-9 Super 81
Origin: USA
Type: short/medium-range transport
Accommodation: flight crew of 2; up to 172 passengers
Powerplant: two 18,500-lb (8391-kg) thrust Pratt & Whitney JT8D-209 turbofans
Performance: maximum speed 575 mph (925 km/h); cruising speed Mach 0.76; range with maximum fuel 3,060 miles (4925 km)
Weights: empty 79,757 lb (36177 kg); maximum take-off 140,000 lb (63503 kg)
Dimensions: span 107 ft 10 in (32.87 m); length 147 ft 10 in (45.06 m); height 29 ft 8 in (9.04 m); wing area 1,270.0 sq ft (117.98 m²)

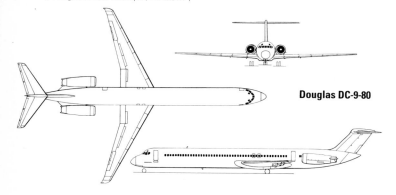

Douglas DC-9-80

Douglas DC-10

Douglas DC-10 Series 30 of Air Afrique, the national airline of the Ivory Coast.

History and Notes

The Douglas Company began development of the DC-10 in March 1966, to meet a requirement of American Airlines for a wide-body transport. Despite competition, the DC-10 was ordered on 19 February 1968, and receipt of a second order in April 1968, from United Airlines, was a signal for production go-ahead. The initial Series 10 for domestic routes, with maximum seating for 380 passengers, was flown first on 29 August 1970, entering service with American Airlines on its Los Angeles-Chicago route on 5 August 1971.

Since then Douglas has developed a range of these transports, first being the Series 15 which is similar to the Series 10 but has more powerful CF6-50C2F engines and operates at a higher gross weight. The intercontinental-range Series 30 has wing span increased by 10 ft (3.05 m), an extra main wheel unit on the fuselage centreline, increased fuel and more powerful engines. The longer-range Series 30ER has even greater fuel capacity, and the intercontinental Series 40 (originally Series 20) differs from the Series 30 in having Pratt & Whitney engines. Model 10CF and 30CF convertible passenger/cargo versions are also available. The DC-10 was evaluated by the USAF for its Advanced Tanker/Cargo Aircraft requirement and its selection for this role was announced on 19 December 1977 under the designation KC-10A Extender, the first entering service on 17 March 1981.

Specification: Douglas DC-10 Series 30
Origin: USA
Type: commercial transport
Accommodation: flight crew of 3, up to 380 passengers
Powerplant: three 52,500-lb (23814-kg) thrust General Electric CF6-50C1 or -50C2 turbofans
Performance: maximum cruising speed 564 mph (908 km/h); normal cruising speed Mach 0.82; service ceiling 33,400 ft (10180 m); range with maximum payload 4,606 miles (7413 km)
Weights: empty 267,197 lb (121199 kg); maximum take-off 580,000 lb (263084 kg)
Dimensions: span 165 ft 4½ in (50.41 m); length 182 ft 1 in (55.50 m); height 58 ft 1 in (17.70 m); wing area 3,958.0 sq ft (367.70 m²)

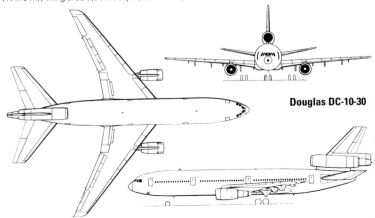

Douglas DC-10-30

EMBRAER EMB-110

EMBRAER EMB-110C Bandeirante of the Brazilian regional airline, TABA.

History and Notes

The EMB-110 is numbered among several of the successful designs that have emanated from Empresa Brasileira de Aeronautica SA (usually abbreviated to EMBRAER) in Brazil. Evolved under guidance from the well-known French designer, Max Holste, the first of three YC-95 prototypes was flown on 26 October 1968. This is a cantilever low-wing monoplane with a conventional fuselage, swept tail surfaces and retractable tricycle landing gear and two Pratt & Whitney Aircraft of Canada PT6A turboprops in wing-mounted nacelles.

Civil transport versions include the EMB-110C, with basic seating for 15 passengers; the seven/eight-passenger EMB-110E executive transport; the EMB-110P 18-passenger commuter; and the EMB-110P2 21-passenger commuter. There is also an EMB-110P1, a quick-change passenger/cargo variant of the EMB-110P2, and available since 1981 are the EMB-110P1/41 and EMB-110P2/41 higher gross weight versions of the P1 and P2 respectively.

EMB-110 Bandeirantes are also in military use; specially equipped for such roles are the EMB-110P1SAR search and rescue aircraft and the EMB-111 maritime surveillance version, both of which are in service with the Brazilian air force under the respective designations of SC-95B and P-95.

Specification: EMBRAER EMB-110P2

Origin: Brazil
Type: commuter transport
Accommodation: flight crew of 2; up to 21 passengers
Powerplant: two 750-shp (559-kW) Pratt & Whitney Aircraft of Canada PT6A-34 turboprops
Performance: maximum cruising speed 257 mph (414 km/h) at 8,000 ft (2440 m); economic cruising speed 208 mph (335 km/h) at 10,000 ft (3050 m); service ceiling 22,500 ft (6860 m); range with fuel reserves 1,243 miles (2000 km)
Weights: empty equipped 7,837 lb (3555 kg); maximum take-off 12,500 lb (5670 kg)
Dimensions: span 50 ft 3½ in (15.33 m); length 49 ft 6½ in (15.10 m); height 16 ft 1¾ in (4.92 m); wing area 313.23 sq ft (29.10 m²)

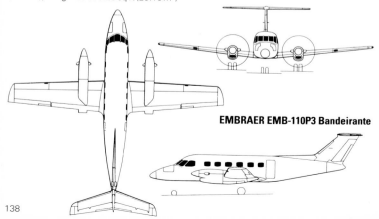

EMBRAER EMB-110P3 Bandeirante

Fokker F.27 Friendship

Fokker F.27 Friendship of Air Tanzania.

History and Notes

Fokker built many fine airliners during the 'between-wars' years, and soon after the end of World War II began looking at the needs of the European airlines. This led to the P.275 design for a 32-seat transport, but by 1952 this had been developed to the larger F.27 with a pressurized fuselage.

A first prototype (PH-NIV) flew on 24 November 1955, powered by Rolls-Royce Dart 507 turboprops. A second prototype, with Dart 511 engines and a lengthened fuselage to seat 32 passengers, was flown on 31 January 1957. Between these dates Fokker concluded arrangements with Fairchild in the USA to build and market the F.27 in North America, resulting in the Fairchild F-27/FH-227.

Fokker production versions comprise the 40/52-seat F.27 Friendship Mk 100 and Mk 200, differing only in powerplant; similar passenger/cargo Mk 300 and Mk 400 Combiplane versions; the Mk 500, a lengthened-fuselage (by 4 ft 11 in/1.50 m) Mk 200 to seat 52/60 passengers; the Mk 600, basically a Mk 200 with large cargo door; and a single Mk 700, a Mk 600 with Mk 100 powerplant. There are also the military Mk 400M and 500M, the Mk 400M aerial survey and, for maritime patrol, the F.27 Maritime. Fokker F.27 sales exceed 550 with some 315 now in service; major operators include Air France, Air New Zealand, Air UK, LADE, Libyan Arab Airlines, Malaysian Airlines System, Merpati Nusantara Airlines and PIA.

Specification: Fokker F.27 Mk 200
Origin: Netherlands
Type: medium-range transport
Accommodation: flight crew of 2; up to 48 passengers
Powerplant: two 2,280-eshp (1700-ekW) Rolls-Royce Dart Mk 536-7R turboprops
Performance: normal cruising speed 298 mph (480 km/h) at 20,000 ft (6095 m); service ceiling 29,500 ft (8990 m); range with 44 passengers and fuel reserves 1,197 miles (1926 km)
Weights: empty operating 26,480 lb (12011 kg); maximum take-off 45,000 lb (20412 kg)
Dimensions: span 95 ft 2 in (29.00 m); length 77 ft 3½ in (23.56 m); height 27 ft 10½ in (8.50 m); wing area 753.50 sq ft (70.00 m²)

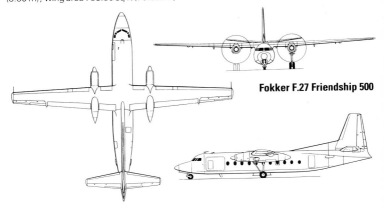

Fokker F.27 Friendship 500

Fokker F.28 Fellowship

Fokker F.28 Fellowship of Aero Peru.

History and Notes

Foreseeing a market for a higher-performance airliner with more capacity than the F.27, Fokker began in 1960 the design of a turbofan-powered short/medium-range transport to complement the F.27. Later designated F.28 Fellowship, this airliner entered production in 1964 with backing from the Netherlands government and risk-sharing partners in West Germany and the UK. Of low-wing monoplane configuration, the F.28 has a circular-section pressurized fuselage, T-tail with swept surfaces, retractable tricycle landing gear and rear-mounted Rolls-Royce Spey turbofans. The first prototype (PH-JHG) was flown on 9 May 1967 and the F.28 entered service on 24 February 1969.

Current versions in 1983 include the Mk 3000, and Mk 4000 with a fuselage lengthened by 7 ft 3 in (2.21 m), seating up to 65 and 85 passengers respectively; the Mk 3000 is available optionally with a 15-seat executive layout. The earlier Mk 1000 and Mk 2000 were respective equivalents of the current production aircraft; the Mk 6000 (2 built) has a standard lengthened fuselage combined with a 4 ft (1.22 m) increase in wing span. Projected Mk 5000 (short fuselage/increased span wings) and Mk 6600 (still longer fuselage) versions were not built.

More than 215 F.28s have been sold and major operators include Linjeflyg AB, Airlines of Western Australia and Garuda Indonesian Airways.

Specification: Fokker F.28 Mk 3000

Origin: Netherlands
Type: short/medium-range transport
Accommodation: flight crew of 2; up to 65 passengers
Powerplant: two 9,900-lb (4491-kg) thrust Rolls-Royce RB.183-2 Spey Mk 555-15P turbofans
Performance: maximum cruising speed 523 mph (842 km/h) at 23,000 ft (7010 m); economic cruising speed 421 mph (678 km/h) at 30,000 ft (9145 m); maximum range with 65 passengers and fuel reserves 1,969 miles (3169 km)
Weights: empty operating 36,994 lb (16780 kg); maximum take-off 72,995 lb (33110 kg)
Dimensions: span 82 ft 3 in (25.07 m); length 89 ft 10¾ in (27.40 m); height 27 ft 9½ in (8.47 m); wing area 850.38 sq ft (79.00 m²)

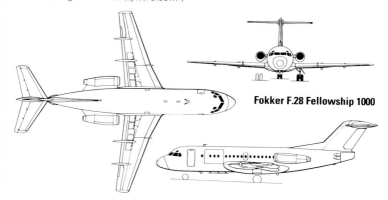

Fokker F.28 Fellowship 1000

Handley Page H.P.R.7 Herald

Handley Page H.P.R.7 Herald of Air UK.

History and Notes

The Handley Page H.P.R.7 Herald medium-range transport prototype (G-AODE) made its first flight on 25 August 1955. A cantilever high-wing monoplane with a circular-section pressurized fuselage, the Herald had a conventional tail unit, retractable tricycle landing gear, and power provided by four 870-hp (649-kW) Alvis Leonides radial engines in wing-mounted nacelles.

Handley Page had expected the Herald to sell to operators in more remote areas, and its easy-to-maintain airframe and powerplant were slanted to such a market. The Herald failed to gain interest, however, for by mid-1955 the capability, reliability and economy of turboprop engines had been demonstrated by aircraft such as the Vickers Viscount. A decision was made in May 1957 to develop a Dart-powered version and only the two prototypes were flown with piston engines, being converted subsequently to turbine power. Produced first was the Herald Series 100 (4 built) which seated 47 passengers; it was followed by the 'stretched' fuselage (by 3 ft 7 in/1.09 m) Series 200 (38 built) to seat 56. Production ended with eight Series 400 military variants for the Royal Malaysian air force, no further examples being built after collapse of the Handley Page company in 1970. Only about 15 Heralds now remain in airline service.

Specification: Handley Page H.P.R.7 Herald Series 200
Origin: UK
Type: medium-range transport
Accommodation: flight crew of 2; up to 56 passengers
Powerplant: two 2,105-eshp (1570-ekW) Rolls-Royce Dart 527 turboprops
Performance: maximum cruising speed 274 mph (441 km/h) at 15,000 ft (4570 m); economic cruising speed 265 mph (426 km/h) at 23,000 ft (7010 m); service ceiling 27,900 ft (8505 m); range with maximum payload 1,110 miles (1786 km)
Weights: empty operating 25,800 lb (11703 kg); maximum take-off 43,000 lb (19504 kg)
Dimensions: span 94 ft 9 in (28.88 m); length 75 ft 6 in (23.01 m); height 24 ft 1 in (7.34 m); wing area 886.00 sq ft (82.31 m^2)

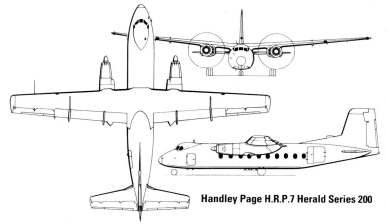

Handley Page H.R.P.7 Herald Series 200

Ilyushin Il-18

Ilyushin Il-18 of the East German line, Interflug.

History and Notes

Aeroflot's need for a medium-range civil transport with greater capacity than the Il-14 led to design of the Il-18, a low-wing monoplane with a circular-section pressurized fuselage, conventional tail unit, retractable tricycle landing gear, and power provided by four wing-mounted 4,000-eshp (2983-ekW) Kuznetsov SN-4 turboprops. The prototype (CCCP-L5811) was flown first on 4 July 1957.

The initial production Il-18s, introduced into service by Aeroflot on 20 April 1959, had seats for 75 passengers. Subsequent versions with layouts revised for up to 84 and 100 passengers were the Il-18B and Il-18V respectively, the latter having some cabin windows repositioned. More extensively developed was the Il-18D (known initially as the Il-18I) with increased fuel tankage, more powerful engines and 'warm weather' seats for up to 122 passengers; this extra capacity was gained by using the large storage area needed for passengers' outer garments during the Russian winter; with its onset, seating capacity reverted to 110. The Il-18E was a generally similar version, but without the additional fuel capacity. About 700 were built, small numbers entering military service, and about 200 remained in airline use in early 1985, the major operators being Aeroflot and CAAC.

Specifically military versions include an ECM or Elint aircraft and an ASW Il-38 which have the NATO reporting names 'Coot-A' and 'May' respectively.

Specification: Ilyushin Il-18D
Origin: USSR
Type: medium/long-range transport
Accommodation: flight crew of 5; up to 122 passengers
Powerplant: four 4,250-eshp (3169-ekW) Ivchenko AI-20M turboprops
Performance: maximum cruising speed 419 mph (675 km/h); maximum operating ceiling 32,810 ft (10000 m); range with maximum payload and fuel reserves 2,299 miles (3700 km)
Weights: empty equipped 77,162 lb (35000 kg); maximum take-off 141,096 lb (64000 kg)
Dimensions: span 122 ft 8½ in (37.40 m); length 117 ft 9½ in (35.90 m); height 33 ft 4½ in (10.17 m); wing area 1,507.00 sq ft (140.00 m²)

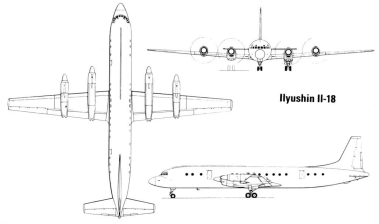

Ilyushin Il-18

Ilyushin Il-62

Ilyushin Il-62 of CSA (Ceskoslovenske Aerolinie).

History and Notes

First announced on 24 September 1962, the Ilyushin Il-62 long-range airliner was designed for use over routes such as Moscow-New York, a distance of some 4,800 miles (7725 km). The prototype (CCCP-06156) was first flown in January 1963, and was a low-wing monoplane with swept wings and tail surfaces, a circular-section pressurized fuselage, retractable tricycle landing gear, and four engines mounted in pairs on each side of the rear fuselage. As first flown the Il-62 was powered by 16,535-lb (7500-kg) thrust Lyulka AL-7 turbojets, but soon afterwards the aircraft was flown with the Kuznetsov turbofans for which it was designed. Passenger accommodation is in two cabins, with maximum seating for 186: 72 forward and 114 rear.

Il-62s entered service with Aeroflot in early 1967, and following initial use on domestic services was introduced on the airline's Moscow-Montreal route on 15 September 1967, then representing the Soviet Union's first long-range four-engine intercontinental jet transport. An improved Il-62M entered service in 1974, incorporating many refinements and more powerful, more fuel efficient Soloviev D-30KU turbofan engines. The most recent version, first announced in 1978, has structural strengthening for operation at higher gross weights, de-rated engines, and a cabin layout for a maximum 195 passengers. About 190 Il-62s now remain in airline service, approximately 75 per cent with Aeroflot.

Specification: Ilyushin Il-62M

Origin: USSR
Type: long-range transport
Accommodation: flight crew of 5; up to 174 passengers
Powerplant: four 25,353-lb (11500-kg) thrust Soloviev D-30KU turbofans
Performance: cruising speed at optimum altitude 510-553 mph (820-890 km/h); range with maximum payload and fuel reserves 4,847 miles (7800 km)
Weights: empty operating 153,001 lb (69400 kg); maximum take-off 363,763 lb (165000 kg)
Dimensions: span 141 ft 8¾ in (43.20 m); length 174 ft 3¼ in (53.12 m); height 40 ft 6¼ in (12.35 m); wing area 3,037.67 sq ft (282.20 m²)

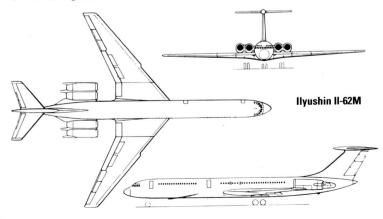

Ilyushin Il-62M

Ilyushin Il-76

Ilyushin Il-76T of Iraqi Airways (note tail gun turret).

History and Notes

In the late 1960s Ilyushin began design studies of a heavy transport aircraft required by Aeroflot for operation in Siberian regions. Designated Il-76, a prototype (CCCP-86712) was flown for the first time on 25 March 1971, and this was exhibited later that year at the Paris Air Show. It has a high-set monoplane wing (to ensure maximum internal capacity) mounted above a circular-section pressurized fuselage, a T-tail with all-swept surfaces, and retractable tricycle landing gear that has a four-wheel nose unit and two main units each with eight wheels. Thus it has 20 wheels with low-pressure tyres to distribute the aircraft's weight over a maximum surface area and, to enhance operational potential, tyre pressures can be adjusted in flight. Power is provided by four Soloviev turbofan engines in underwing pods. The all-important loading operations take place via two large clamshell type doors, an upward hinged panel and a downward-hinged loading ramp being incorporated in the upswept rear fuselage.

Production Il-76Ts began to enter service with Aeroflot in early 1983, and in 1981 this airline was operating about 80; others serve with Iraqi Airways. An Il-76M military transport, of which about 140 are believed to be in service with the Soviet air force, differs by having a rear turret. The type is also being developed for use in AWACS and inflight-refuelling tanker roles.

Specification: Ilyushin Il-76T

Origin: USSR
Type: medium/long-range freight transport
Accommodation: flight crew of 7
Powerplant: four 26,455-lb (12000-kg) thrust Soloviev D-30KP turbofans
Performance: maximum speed 528 mph (850 km/h); cruising speed 466-497 mph (750-800 km/h); range with maximum payload 3,107 miles (5000 km)
Weights: maximum payload 88,185 lb (40000 kg); maximum take-off 374,786 lb (170000 kg)
Dimensions: span 165 ft 8¼ in (50.50 m); length 152 ft 10¼ in (46.59 m); height 48 ft 5 in (14.76 m); wing area 3,229.28 sq ft (300.00 m²)

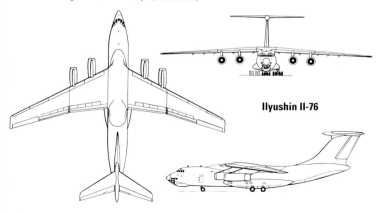

Ilyushin Il-76

Ilyushin Il-86

Ilyushin Il-86 of Aeroflot.

Ilyushin Il-86 of Aeroflot.

History and Notes

A first intimation that the Soviet aerospace industry was developing a wide-body transport came at the 1971 Paris Air Show. Little was then known of its proposed configuration, but the first pictures of the Ilyushin Il-86 prototype (CCCP-86000), which made its maiden flight on 22 December 1976, showed it to be similar to the European Airbus Industrie A300 except for having four instead of two underwing-mounted turbofan engines, and for having a third main landing gear unit similar to that of the Douglas DC-10 Series 30 and 40. The Il-86 has accommodation for a maximum of 350 passengers, split between three cabins which are separated by wardrobes. Access to this aircraft is unique, being via three lower-deck airstair type doors which enable the aircraft to dispense with conventional airport loading/unloading bridges. These airstairs reach down to ground level and, after boarding, passengers can deposit their baggage in lower-deck stowage positions before climbing one of three fixed internal staircases to the passenger cabins.

What is believed to be the initial production aircraft flew on 24 October 1977, but it was not until 24 September 1979 that Aeroflot took delivery of its first Il-86. Scheduled services were started on 26 December 1980, initially between Moscow and Tashkent. About 50 are believed to be in service.

Specification: Ilyushin Il-86
Origin: USSR
Type: medium-range transport
Accommodation: flight crew of 5; up to 350 passengers
Powerplant: four 28,660-lb (13000 kg) thrust Kuznetsov NK-86 turbofans
Performance: (estimated) cruising speed 559-590 mph (900-950 km/h) at optimum altitude; range with 88,185 lb (40000 kg) payload 2,237 miles (3600 km)
Weights: maximum payload 92,594 lb (42000 kg); maximum take-off 454,152 lb (206000 kg)
Dimensions: span 157 ft 8¼ in (48.06 m); length 195 ft 4 in (59.54 m); height 51 ft 10½ in (15.81 m); wing area 3,444.56 sq ft (320.00 m²)

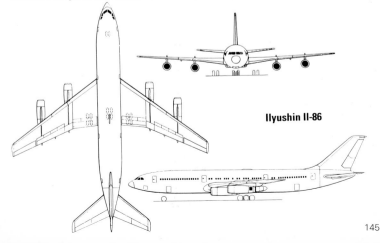

Ilyushin Il-86

Lockheed L-1011 TriStar

Lockheed L-1011-200 TriStar of Saudia.

History and Notes

Lockheed's L-1011 TriStar was designed to meet the same American Airlines' requirement that had initiated production of the Douglas DC-10, to which the TriStar is generally similar in configuration, including the disposition of its three-engined powerplant. Production began in early 1968, after orders for 144 aircraft had been received, and the first was flown on 17 November 1970. At this point both Lockheed in the USA and Rolls-Royce in the UK ran into serious economic problems, requiring assistance from their respective governments and the renegotiation of contracts before production could be resumed, and it was not until 14 April 1972 that certification was gained, with the first scheduled service flown by Eastern Air Lines on 26 April 1972.

This basic TriStar was designated L-1011-1 and was powered by three 42,000-lb (19051-kg) thrust Rolls-Royce RB.211-22B turbofans. It was followed by an extended-range L-1011-100 with increased fuel tankage, and later by an extended-range L-1011-200 with more powerful RB.211-524 engines giving improved performance for operation in 'hot and high' areas. Construction of all versions, including the L-1011-500 totalled 250 when production ended in 1983.

Specification: Lockheed L-1011-200 TriStar
Origin: USA
Type: commercial transport
Accommodation: flight crew of 3; up to 400 passengers
Powerplant: three 48,000-lb or 50,000-lb (21772-kg or 22680-kg) thrust Rolls-Royce RB.211-524 or -524B/B4 turbofans respectively
Performance: maximum cruising speed 605 mph (974 km/h) at 30,000 ft (9145 m); economic cruising speed 553 mph (890 km/h) at 35,000 ft (10670 m); range with maximum passengers and fuel reserves 4,145 miles (6671 km)
Weights: empty operating 248,400 lb (112672 kg); maximum take-off 466,000 lb (211374 kg)
Dimensions: span 155 ft 4 in (47.35 m); length 177 ft 8½ in (54.17 m); height 55 ft 4 in (16.87 m); wing area 3,456.0 sq ft (321.06 m²)

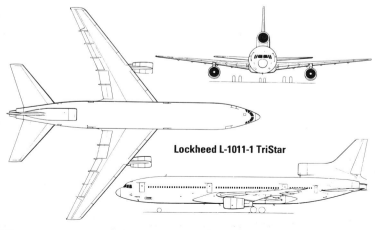

Lockheed L-1011-1 TriStar

Lockheed L-1011-500 TriStar

Lockheed L-1011-500 TriStar of British West Indian Airways.

History and Notes

It was intended that when testing of the first TriStar (N1011) had ended it should be refurbished to airline standards. However, the company found a need to retain it for development and it became known as the Advanced TriStar. It has modifications and equipment that includes active aileron control, an all-moving tailplane, automatic brakes, automatic take-off thrust, extended wingtips and advanced avionics and systems. Added to the starboard side of the instrument panel in late 1981 were three full-colour CRT displays to test pilot reactions and evaluate different information formats.

Airline interest in a long-range version of the TriStar led to the L-1011-500, which began flight tests in October 1978. It differs from early production versions by having a shorter fuselage (by 13 ft 6 in/4.11 m), reducing internal seating to a maximum of 330 passengers. This smaller payload allows for increased fuel, carried in added centre-section tanks. There are also variations in interior layout, and the extended wingtips/active ailerons tested on the Advanced TriStar became standard on the L-1011-500 in 1981. Major operators of TriStars of all versions are Air Canada, All Nippon, British Airways, Delta Air Lines, Eastern Air Lines, Saudia and TWA.

Specification: Lockheed L-1011-500 TriStar
Origin: USA
Type: long-range commercial transport
Accommodation: flight crew of 3; up to 330 passengers
Powerplant: three 50,000-lb (22680-kg) thrust Rolls-Royce RB.211-524B/B4 turbofans
Performance: maximum cruising speed 605 mph (974 km/h) at 30,000 ft (9145 m); economic cruising speed 553 mph (890 km/h) at 35,000 ft (10670 m); service ceiling 43,000 ft (13105 m); range with maximum passengers and fuel reserves 6,154 miles (9904 km)
Weights: empty operating 245,400 lb (111312 kg); maximum take-off 510,000 lb (231332 kg)
Dimensions: span 164 ft 4 in (50.09 m); length 164 ft 2½ in (50.05 m); height 55 ft 4 in (16.87 m); wing area 3541.0 sq ft (328.96 m²)

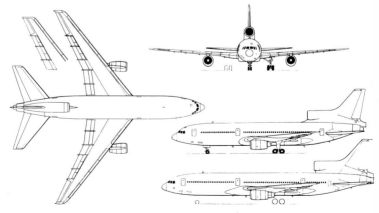

Lockheed L-1011-500 TriStar (lower side and scrap views: L-1011-100)

NAMC YS-11

NAMC YS-11 of Toa Domestic Airlines.

History and Notes

In May 1957 a Transport Aircraft Development Association was created in Japan to design a medium-range civil airliner. With this task completed the Nihon Aircraft Manufacturing Company (NAMC) was established on 1 June 1959 as a management and sales medium to co-ordinate the activities of the six member companies which were to build the components for this YS-11 aircraft. They comprised Fuji, Kawasaki, Mitsubishi, Nippi, Shin Meiwa and Showa, with Mitsubishi responsible also for final assembly.

Activities began with the construction of two prototypes, the first being flown on 30 August 1962. Certification was gained on 25 August 1964 and production deliveries began in March 1965. In configuration the YS-11 is a low-wing monoplane with a circular-section pressurized fuselage, retractable tricycle landing gear and two wing-mounted turboprops. Initial production version was the YS-11-100, followed by three similar versions certificated at a higher gross weight, comprising YS-11A-200 passenger, YS-11A-300 mixed passenger/cargo, and YS-11A-400 all-cargo versions. Subsequently, equivalent YS-11A-500, YS-11A-600, and YS-11A-700 versions became available with the maximum take-off weight increased by 1,102 lb (500 kg). Production ended in 1974 after 182 aircraft had been built, and of this total about 120 remain in service with Airborne Express, All Nippon Airways, MidPacific Airlines and Toa Domestic as major operators.

Specification: NAMC YS-11A-200

Origin: Japan
Type: short/medium-range transport
Accommodation: flight crew of 2; up to 60 passengers
Powerplant: two 3,060-eshp (2282-ekW) Rolls-Royce Dart Mk 542-10K turboprops
Performance: maximum cruising speed 291 mph (468 km/h) at 15,000 ft (4570 m); economic cruising speed 281 mph (452 km/h) at 20,000 ft (6095 m); service ceiling 22,900 ft (6980 m); range with maximum payload 680 miles (1094 km)
Weights: empty operating 33,993 lb (15419 kg); maximum take-off 54,013 lb (24500 kg)
Dimensions: span 104 ft 11¾ in (32.00 m); length 86 ft 3½ in (26.30 m); height 29 ft 5½ in (8.98 m); wing area 1,020.45 sq ft (94.80 m²)

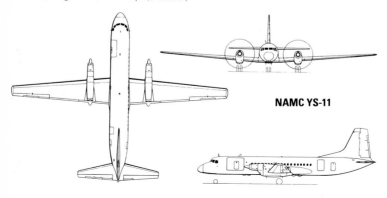

NAMC YS-11

Saab-Fairchild 340

Saab-Fairchild 340 of the Swiss regional airline Crossair.

History and Notes

In recent years there have been several aircraft developed by international collaboration between manufacturers. The growing complexity and cost of new high-technology aircraft has placed even greater emphasis on the need for such associations, but that formed between Saab-Scania in Sweden and Fairchild Industries in the USA is, so far, unique. It is the first to unite European and US aerospace industries in the development of a civil transport aircraft.

Known as the Saab-Fairchild 340, this aircraft is designed for easy maintenance and quick turn-arounds without reliance upon airport ground-handling equipment. It has new-generation fuel-efficient wing-mounted turboprop engines and is configured as a cantilever low-wing monoplane with a circular-section pressurized fuselage, conventional tail unit and retractable tricycle landing gear with twin wheels on each unit. It is available in airline and corporate versions with standard seating for 35 and 16 passengers respectively.

The first prototype was rolled out on schedule at Linkoping, Sweden on 27 October 1982 and made its first flight on 25 January 1983; certification was gained on 30 May 1984 and the first customer aircraft was delivered to Crossair of Switzerland which operated the first revenue service on 15 June 1984. Orders and options total more than 100 aircraft, and about 15 were in airline service in early 1985.

Specification: Saab-Fairchild 340 Commuter

Origin: International
Type: short-range transport
Accommodation: flight crew of 2 or 3; up to 35 passengers
Powerplant: two 1,630-shp (1215-kw) General Electric CT7-5A turboprops
Performance: maximum cruising speed 315 mph (508 km/h) at 15,000 ft (4570 m); economic cruising speed 290 mph (467 km/h); service ceiling 25,000 ft (7620 m). There are no replace figures for this as range is not now quoted
Weights: empty operating 17,000 lb (7711 kg); maximum take-off 27,000 lb (12247 kg)
Dimensions: span 70 ft 4 in (21.44 m); length 64 ft 8 in (19.71 m); height 22 ft 6½ in (6.87 m); wing area 450.0 sq ft (41.81 m²)

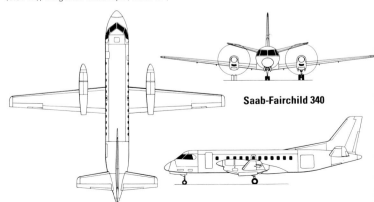

Saab-Fairchild 340

Shorts 330

Shorts 330 of US commuter airline Command Airways.

History and Notes

It was once suggested that sales of the Short Skyvan might reach 1,000, but with only about nine aircraft per year built since 1966 it now seems unlikely that 25 per cent of this figure will be realized. The reason is that its market prospects are limited by capacity/performance: if either factor could be increased significantly then, theoretically, so would sales figures.

This thinking led Shorts to develop an aircraft similar to the Skyvan, but with seats for 30 passengers. The resulting Shorts 330 has many features of its predecessor, including its wide cabin, but one that is increased in length by 12 ft 5 in (3.78 m). The same overall configuration is retained, but retractable tricycle landing gear and improved lines help ensure that its two Pratt & Whitney PT6A turboprop engines can provide better performance. The first of two prototypes (G-BSBH) was flown on 22 August 1974 and initial deliveries made in June 1976. Three versions were available in 1985, the standard passenger 330-200, a Sherpa civil freighter which has a Skyvan-type rear loading door, and the 330-UTT military utility tactical transport. A total of 115 orders and options for all versions have been received, and of this number about 90 have been delivered. major operators are Command Airways, Mississippi Valley Airlines, Pennsylvania Airlines and Suburban Airlines.

Specification: Shorts 330-200

Origin: UK
Type: short-range transport
Accommodation: flight crew of 2; up to 30 passengers
Powerplant: two 1,198-shp (893-kW) Pratt & Whitney Aircraft of Canada PT6A-45R turboprops
Performance: maximum cruising speed 218 mph (351 km/h) at 10,000 ft (3050 m); economic cruising speed 184 mph (296 km/h) at 10,000 ft (3050 m); range with 30 passengers 553 miles (890 km)
Weights: empty equipped 14,700 lb (6668 kg); maximum take-off 22,900 lb (10387 kg)
Dimensions: span 74 ft 8 in (22.76 m); length 58 ft 0½ in (17.69 m); height 16 ft 3 in (4.95 m); wing area 453.0 sq ft (42.08 m²)

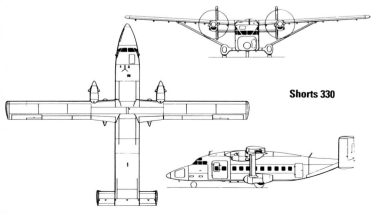

Shorts 330

Shorts 360

Shorts 360 of Air Ecosse used for British postal duties.

History and Notes

Shorts announced on 10 July 1980 the introduction of a 'stretched' development of its Shorts 330, reflecting the buoyancy of the commuter airline market despite a general recession affecting so many airline operators. The type is designated Shorts 360, the numerical suffix indicating the 36-seat capacity of this new aircraft, which differs from its immediate predecessor in several respects. It retains the same basic configuration and, because it is intended for operation over short stage lengths and does not need cabin pressurization, has the same roomy cabin interior with dimensions of 6 ft 6 in (1.98 m) in height and width. It differs in having the fuselage lengthened by 3 ft 0 in (0.91 m), strengthened wing bracing struts and wing outer panels, and fuel-efficient engines of greater power. Most conspicuous of the changes is the adoption of a revised rear fuselage, incorporating a conventional tail unit with single fin and rudder. Intended to reduce drag, and hence increase fuel efficiency, this also provides greater baggage capacity.

The Shorts 360 prototype (G-ROOM), then powered by PT6A-45 turboprops, was flown on 1 June 1981. The intended PT6A-65R engines were installed subsequently and, following the first flight of a production aircraft on 19 August 1982, certification was gained on 3 September 1982. The first of four for Suburban Airlines of Reading, Pennsylvania entered service in November 1982, and Shorts have now received orders and options for more than 60 of these aircraft.

Specification: Shorts 360

Origin: UK
Type: commuter transport
Accommodation: flight crew of 2; up to 36 passengers
Powerplant: two 1,327-shp (990-kW) Pratt & Whitney Aircraft of Canada PT6A-65R turboprops
Performance: cruising speed 243 mph (391 km/h); range with 36 passengers and fuel reserves 265 miles (426 km)
Weights: empty operating 16,600 lb (7530 kg); maximum take-off 25,700 lb (11657 kg)
Dimensions: span 74 ft 10 in (22.81 m); length 70 ft 10 in (21.59 m); height 23 ft 8 in (7.21 m); wing area 453.0 sq ft (42.08 m²)

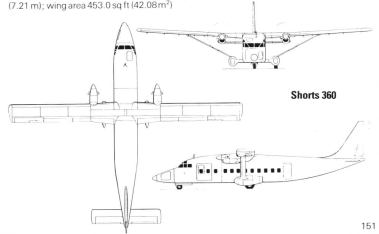

Shorts 360

Tupolev Tu-134

Tupolev Tu-134 of LOT Polish Airlines.

History and Notes

Tupolev's bureau was probably elated by the success of Tu-104s and Tu-124s in use by Aeroflot, but must have been concerned that neither had attracted any export orders. This resulted in a version of the Tu-124 with a more interesting interior layout. Allocated the provisional designation Tu-124A, the aircraft retained wings, fuselage and landing gear that were generally similar, but in two aspects this aircraft was completely different. Firstly, the turbofan powerplant was removed from the wings, ensuring 'clean' aerodynamic surfaces unaffected by engine intake/efflux and the airflow around nacelles, and mounted instead on the rear fuselage. Secondly, this resulted in replacement of the conventional tail unit by a T-tail, and because of these changes the Tu-124A was redesignated Tu-134.

The first Tu-134, powered by two Soloviev D-30 turbofans and seating up to 72 passengers, entered service with Aeroflot in September 1967, but the Tu-134A, introduced in 1970, had a fuselage lengthened by 6 ft 10½ in (2.10 m) to seat up to 84. With this aircraft Tupolev achieved some export success and it has been built in larger numbers. The most recent version, which probably began to enter service during 1982, is the Tu-134B with seats for up to 90 passengers. Production is estimated as 650-700, the majority in current service, with Aeroflot and Interflug as major operators.

Specification: Tupolev Tu-134A

Origin: USSR
Type: short/medium-range transport
Accommodation: flight crew of 3; up to 84 passengers
Powerplant: two 14,991-lb (6800-kg) thrust Soloviev D-30 Srs II turbofans
Performance: maximum cruising speed 550 mph (885 km/h); economic cruising speed 466 mph (750 km/h); service ceiling 39,010 ft (11890 m); range with maximum payload 1,174 miles (1890 km)
Weights: empty operating 64,044 lb (29050 kg); maximum take-off 103,617 lb (47000 kg)
Dimensions: span 95 ft 1¾ in (29.00 m); length 121 ft 6¾ in (37.05 m); height 30 ft 0 in (9.15 m); wing area 1,370.29 sq ft (127.30 m²)

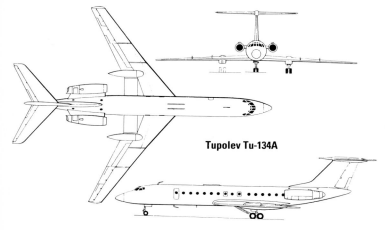

Tupolev Tu-134A

Tupolev Tu-154

Tupolev Tu-154B-2 operated by Malev.

History and Notes

In the mid-1960s Tupolev's bureau received a challenging requirement, the design of an aircraft to replace Antonov An-10s, Ilyushin Il-18s and Tupolev Tu-104s in service. Such an airliner needed to combine the secondary field performance of the An-10, range capability of the Il-18 and speed of the Tu-104. The resulting Tu-154 resembles but is slightly larger than the Boeing 727, and shares the same rear-mounted three-engined layout. It is a low-wing monoplane with a circular-section pressurized fuselage, T-tail and retractable tricycle landing gear which has a six-wheel bogie on each main unit. The initial Tu-154s evaluated in 1971 were powered by 20,944-lb (9500-kg) thrust Kuznetsov NK-8-2 turbofans.

Aeroflot's first Tu-154 services began on 8 February 1972. Since then the improved Tu-154A and Tu-154B have been developed, both with more powerful engines, greater fuel capacity and performance/reliability refinements. The Tu-154B differs by having a slightly longer cabin, without change in fuselage dimensions, to accommodate up to 169 passengers. Tu-154As and Tu-154Bs are believed to have entered service in 1975 and 1978 respectively. Since then a Tu-154B-2, incorporating refinements, and a mixed passenger/cargo Tu-154M have been reported. Production of all versions is believed to be over 600, the majority still remaining in service, with Aeroflot, Balkan Bulgarian Airlines and Tarom the major operators.

Specification: Tupolev Tu-154A

Origin: USSR
Type: medium/long-range transport
Accommodation: flight crew of 3 or 4; up to 168 passengers
Powerplant: three 23,149-lb (10500-kg) thrust Kuznetsov NK-8-2U turbofans
Performance: cruising speed 559 mph (900 km/h) at 39,370 ft (12000 m); range with maximum payload and fuel reserves 1,709 miles (2750 km)
Weights: empty operating 111,940 lb (50775 kg); maximum take-off 207,235 lb (94000 kg)
Dimensions: span 123 ft 2¼ in (37.55 m); length 157 ft 1¾ in (47.90 m); height 37 ft 4¾ in (11.40 m); wing area 2,168.46 sq ft (201.45 m²)

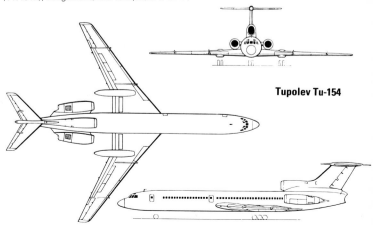

Tupolev Tu-154

Vickers Viscount

Vickers Viscount of British Midland Airways.

Vickers Viscount of British Midland Airways.

History and Notes

Named originally Viceroy, but renamed Viscount after India became an independent state within the British Commonwealth, the Vickers Type 630 prototype was first flown on 16 July 1948. Then powered by four 1,380-eshp (1029-ekW) Rolls-Royce RDa.l Mk 502 turboprop engines, providing impressive and smooth performance, the Type 630 failed to attract any interest because of its 32-seat capacity. Fortunately a more powerful version of the Dart became available, leading to a Type 700 Viscount which was acceptable to British European Airways (BEA) and could seat up to 43 passengers. The first production Viscount for BEA was flown on 20 August 1952, certificated on 17 April 1953, and was used to inaugurate Viscount services between London and Cyprus on the following day.

A mass of orders for this attractive transport followed, including significant numbers for North America, and it seemed that at last the British industry had broken into the American market. Such hopes were premature, but the Viscount retains the record of being the UK's most extensively built airliner, production totalling 444. These included the Type 700D seating up to 59, the lengthened fuselage (by 3 ft 10 in/1.17 m) Type 800 seating up to 71, and the type 810 for operation at higher gross weight. Only about 50 of these aircraft now remain in service, used by more than 20 airlines, with British Air Ferries the major operator.

Specification: Vickers Type 810 Viscount
Origin: UK
Type: short/medium-range transport
Accommodation: flight crew of 2 or 3; up to 71 passengers
Powerplant: four 2,100-eshp (1566-ekW) Rolls-Royce Dart RDa.7/1 Mk 525 turboprops
Performance: maximum cruising speed 350 mph (563 km/h) at 20,000 ft (6095 m); service ceiling 25,000 ft (7620 m); range with maximum payload 1,725 miles (2776 km)
Weights: empty operating 41,565 lb (18854 kg); maximum take-off 72,500 lb (32885 kg)
Dimensions: span 93 ft 8½ in (28.56 m); length 85 ft 8 in (26.11 m); height 26 ft 9 in (8.15 m); wing area 963.0 sq ft (89.46 m²)

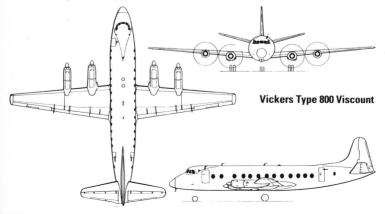

Vickers Type 800 Viscount

The most extensively built British airliner was the Vickers Viscount, and these pioneer turboprop aircraft still soldier on around the world. A major user is British Midland Airways.

Yakovlev Yak-40

Yakovlev Yak-40 of Balkan Bulgarian Airlines.

History and Notes

Designed in the early 1960s as a feederliner to replace Lisunov Li-2s (Soviet-built DC-3s) in Aeroflot service, the Yak-40 feederliner was destined to be built in large numbers if it met Aeroflot's requirements successfully. To fulfil the role it needed to operate effectively from grass airfields or semi-prepared strips, dictating a design which incorporated high-lift lightly-loaded wings, plus the added safety of three- rather than two-engined powerplant. A cantilever low-wing monoplane with a circular-section fuselage, T-tail, retractable tricycle landing gear and rear-mounted Ivchenko AI-25 turbofans, the first prototype made its maiden flight on 21 October 1966.

Production aircraft were first used for revenue services by Aeroflot on 30 September 1968 and when production ended, during 1979-80, it was believed that close on 1,000 had been built for Aeroflot and for export. Accommodation on the flight deck allows for a crew of two or three, and a variety of cabin arrangements caters for a maximum of 32 passengers. For operation from airfields with minimum facilities, the Yak-40 has a ventral door with airstair at the rear of the cabin, and an auxiliary power unit mounted in the fin fairing makes the aircraft independent of ground facilities for starting and the maintenance of air-conditioning/heating. Well over 700 Yak-40s still remain in service, the major operators being Aeroflot, Balkan Bulgarian Airlines and CSA Czechoslovak Airlines.

Specification: Yakovlev Yak-40

Origin: USSR
Type: short-range transport
Accommodation: flight crew of 2 or 3; up to 32 passengers
Powerplant: three 3,307-lb (1500-kg) thrust Ivchenko AI-25 turbofans
Performance: maximum cruising speed 342 mph (550 km/h) at 23,000 ft (7010 m); range with 32 passengers and fuel reserves 901 miles (1450 km)
Weights: empty 20,723 lb (9400 kg); maximum take-off 35,274 lb (16000 kg)
Dimensions: span 82 ft 0¼ in (25.00 m); length 66 ft 9½ in (20.36 m); height 21 ft 3¾ in (6.50 m); wing area 753.5 sq ft (70.00 m²)

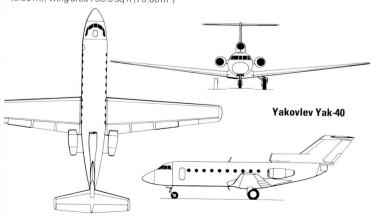

Yakovlev Yak-40

Yakovlev Yak-42

Yakovlev Yak-42 in the colours of Aeroflot.

History and Notes

With the requirement for a medium-range transport to replace Ilyushin Il-18s and Tupolev Tu-134s then in Aeroflot service, Yakovlev decided to benefit from its considerable experience with the Yak-40. From it the company has developed a larger-capacity version of generally similar configuration under the designation Yak-42. The first of three prototypes, with 11° wing sweep, was flown on 7 March 1975; the second and third prototypes had 23° wing sweep and, following flight evaluation, the latter configuration was chosen for production aircraft. The Yak-42 also differs from the Yak-40 by having all-swept surfaces for the T-tail, twin wheels on each landing gear unit and, of course, more powerful turbofan engines.

The first production aircraft began to enter scheduled service with Aeroflot in late 1980, these having a single passenger cabin with seats for a maximum of 120 passengers. An alternative 100-passenger local-service layout is available, this having forward and rear carry-on baggage and coat storage compartments, and it is expected that a 'stretched' 140-passenger version will be certificated in due course. There are provisions for a convertible passenger/cargo interior and the whole accommodation is pressurized and air-condition. It is believed that about 60 are now in service with Aeroflot.

Specification: Yakovlev Yak-42
Origin: USSR
Type: medium-range transport
Accommodation: flight crew of 2; up to 120 passengers
Powerplant: three 14,330-lb (6500-kg) thrust Lotarev D-36 turbofans
Performance: maximum cruising speed 503 mph (810 km/h) at 25,000 ft (7620 m); economic cruising speed 466 mph (750 km/h); range with maximum payload 559 miles (900 km)
Weights: empty 63,846 lb (28960 kg); maximum take-off 117,947 lb (53,500 kg)
Dimensions: span 112 ft 2½ in (34.20 m); length 119 ft 4¼ in (36.38 m); height 32 ft 1¾ in (9.80 m); wing area 1,614.64 sq ft (150.00 m²)

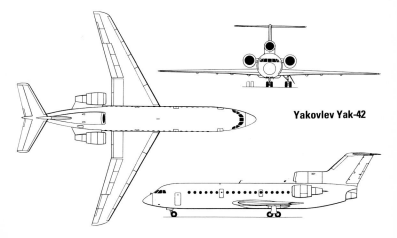

Yakovlev Yak-42

INDEX

Picture acknowledgements

The publishers would like to thank the following individuals and organizations for their help in supplying photographs for this book.

Page 6: U. Schaefer Slides (via J.R. Roach). **7:** T. Lakmaker (via J.R. Roach). **9:** J.R. Roach. **10:** Airbus Industrie. **11:** Austin J. Brown. **12:** H. Oehninger/AeroGem Slides (via J.R. Roach). **14:** Fokker. **15:** Aérospatiale. **16:** Air India. **18:** U. Schaefer slides (via J.R. Roach). **19:** J.R. Roach. **21:** Alaska Airlines. **22:** Austin J. Brown. **23:** J.R. Roach, All Nippon Airways. **25:** Boeing. **27:** Austrian Airlines. **28:** J.R. Roach. **30:** P. Jary (via J.R. Roach). **31:** U. Schaefer slides (via J.R. Roach). **33:** P. Jary (via J.R. Roach). **34:** McDonnell-Douglas. **37:** Bob A. Munro. **39:** T. Lakmaker (via J.R. Roach). **40:** McDonnell-Douglas. **41:** McDonnell—Douglas. **42:** AeroGem Slides (via J.R. Roach). **44:** J.R. Roach; **45:** Lockheed. **49:** Austin J. Brown. **50:** J.R. Roach, Ethiopian Airlines. **52:** J.R. Roach. **53:** J.R. Roach. **54:** Airbus Industrie. **55:** J.R. Roach. **56:** Boeing. **58:** Iran Air. **60:** Japan Air Lines. **61:** Austin J. Brown. **62:** KLM. **64:** J.R. Roach. **65:** Austin J. Brown. **67:** Airbus Industrie. **68:** Austin J. Brown. **69:** Austin J. Brown. **70:** Mexicana. **72:** McDonnell-Douglas. **74:** McDonnell-Douglas. **75:** Olympic Airways. **77:** McDonnell-Douglas. **78:** McDonnell-Douglas. **79:** M.J. Axe. **81:** Airbus Industrie. **82:** Qantas. **83:** Austin J. Brown. **84:** P. Van Damme (via J.R. Roach). **85:** Saudia. **86:** A. Holstrom/AeroGem Slides (via J.R. Roach). **87:** Singapore Airlines. **88:** J.R. Roach. **91:** Swissair. **92:** P. Jary (via J.R. Roach). **93:** A. Holstrom/AeroGem Slides (via J.R. Roach). **94:** J.R. Roach. **95:** Airbus Industrie. **97:** J.R. Roach, Airbus Industrie. **98:** Transbrasil. **99:** T. Lakmaker (via J.R. Roach). **100:** McDonnell-Douglas. **100:** J.R. Roach. **103:** Boeing. **104:** McDonnell-Douglas. **105:** J.R. Roach. **107:** Austin J. Brown. **108:** U. Schaefer Slides (via J.R. Roach). **115:** Austin J. Brown. **119:** Iberia. **155:** British Midland Airways.